Dow vs. California

The Conservation Foundation is a nonprofit research and communications organization dedicated to encouraging human conduct to sustain and enrich life on earth. Since its founding in 1948, it has attempted to provide intellectual leadership in the cause of wise management of the earth's resources.

Dow vs. California:
A Turning Point in the
Envirobusiness Struggle

Christopher J. Duerksen

 The Conservation Foundation
Washington, D.C.

Dow vs. California: A Turning Point in the Envirobusiness Struggle

Copyright © 1982 by The Conservation Foundation

Library of Congress Catalog Card Number: 82-19942

International Standard Book Number: 0-89164-076-2

Cover design by Sally A. Janin

Typeset by VIP Systems, Inc., Alexandria, Virginia

Printed by Todd/Allan Printing Company, Washington, D.C.

The Conservation Foundation
1717 Massachusetts Avenue, N.W.
Washington, D.C. 20036

To Jan,
for helping me keep it in perspective

Contents

Maps, a chart, and photographs appear between pages 66 and 67

Contents

Foreword

In 1977 we at The Conservation Foundation began hearing rumblings that the environmental regulatory system constructed in the early 1970s had become so complex and burdensome that it was stifling needed capital investment and economic growth, particularly in the manufacturing sector. Environmentalists hotly denied these claims, but evidence on both sides was lacking. In 1978, with generous assistance from the German Marshall Fund of the United States, the Ford Foundation, and the Richard King Mellon Foundation, we assembled a team under the direction of Senior Associate Chris Duerksen to get at the truth. Were environmental regulations really that important in the siting of new industry? Were they putting American industry at a competitive disadvantage? Could the process be improved without sacrificing environmental goals?

These questions guided us over the next three years. Duerksen and other members of the multidisciplinary team, which included economist Robert Healy, political scientists H. Jeffrey Leonard and Richard Liroff, and lawyer Michael Mantell, undertook statistical analyses, and conducted surveys and scores of interviews in their search for evidence. In an effort to better understand how the siting process worked in practice, as opposed to theory, they also undertook case studies of several highly publicized industrialized siting disputes that had taken place in the United States during the 1970s. That is where the Dow case fits in.

In January 1977, Dow Chemical announced that it was dropping plans to build a huge $500-million petrochemical facility on the Sacramento River near San Francisco because of environmental regulatory roadblocks. The shock waves rocked Sacramento and the Brown Administration, eventually spreading throughout the country to corporate headquarters and to Capitol Hill. Had the country gone too far in its quest to protect the environment? Looking back, it is clear that the Dow case was a turning point in the environmental movement. The halcyon days of the environmental decade were coming to an end. Never again would environmental regulations pass muster without painful scrutiny, with an eye toward the economy and jobs.

But the story of what really happened to Dow in California has never been told. Business publications pointed an accusing finger at Jerry Brown and environmentalists, claiming they were killing the golden goose in the Golden State, setting a bad example for the rest of the nation. Environmentalists retorted that it was not they who had blocked the project but poor corporate planning which had disregarded basic environmental as well as local planning and zoning concerns.

In all the confusion and acrimony, the real lessons of Dow were ignored, ones that can guide us as we enter the 1980s with a difficult task of balancing ahead of us. Our own work on other projects documents the fact that the environment is far from secure and that challenges lie ahead; yet no one can doubt the need for economic growth with unemployment hovering near depression levels. The Dow case makes clear that everyone—environmentalists, industry, the regulators—has an opportunity to make the process work better without sacrificing our environment in the process. The burden to improve the system rests not with one institution or group; it is a common one. The *are* practical measures we can take to reduce the delays and remove some of the uncertainties which have characterized new industrial development in the United States. These measures are set out in a forthcoming report from our project.

This is not that report. This is a book about one significant encounter between traditional industrial expectations and untried young environmental policies. It is decidedly not a success story. Rather it is a chronicle of poor communication and inexcusable waste of time and money in reaching a decision to retain the status quo. But this story is not unique or unprecedented. Unfortunately, many of America's new industrial developments have been sited, or not sited, in much the same way as the Dow plant proposal was handled in California. Because of the seriousness of the issue for both our environment and our economy, we have decided to treat the case in some detail.

The Dow book tells a story. Duerksen, a lawyer, has applied a reporter's eye to a complex series of events, analyzed their causes, set out their consequences, and produced a lively and fast-moving account. In the process, he has injected life and drama into a subject usually treated as dull and arcane, the purview of experts.

William K. Reilly
President
The Conservation Foundation

Preface

When I came to The Conservation Foundation in 1978 to run our Industrial Siting Project, I had no idea I would end up writing this book. I stumbled onto the Dow vs. California controversy midstream in research, in the course of (as our project brochure says) looking for ''ways to expedite industrial siting decisions while maintaining environmental standards.'' Now, that is, frankly, a weighty, dry-sounding subject, probably of real interest only to those who have chosen to put themselves to the torture of trying to understand environmental laws and how they work (or fail to).

The Dow case was a revelation to me, a lawyer, looking for the kinds of answers that law school had trained me to dig for. Here I found the people and the places behind the dry language of regulations and law, the nuances of events impossible to capture in a hard-eyed, think-tank type approach to a technical issue. It taught me much about how things really work beyond the Potomac, beyond the statute books and corporate headquarters.

It also reaffirmed my feeling that we Americans are an increasingly odd breed in a cynical world. We see a problem and, instead of hand-wringing, energetically spring to set things right. We fight among ourselves, but can look back and try to find what we learned on the positive side and then drink a beer together afterwards. Perhaps most importantly, I saw firsthand that a deep current of concern about our environment runs through the citizenry of this country, from corporate president to small farmer, from government regulator to small-town politician. Not that we're all environmentalists, and to be sure there are the recalcitrant, a few of whom you will meet in the following pages. But events and attitudes have passed these people by. That fact gives me much hope.

I cannot begin to thank everyone who helped me get from my first interview back in the summer of 1979 to this book. My good friends Ann Felber and Bob McCoy are most responsible for its seeing the light of day. If they had not snatched it from oblivion at the bottom of one of my file drawers, it would now be buried in some storage box. Jeff Cohn massaged the manuscript mightily to make me sound lucid, and Laura O'Sullivan, Tony Brown, and Carolyn Lynn typed innumerable drafts and now can recite chapters by heart. All the while, strong support and encouragement from Marianne Ginsburg of the German Marshall Fund helped keep my work on track.

Of course, the book would not have been possible without the patient help of all the players in the Dow case as well as others. Dean Misczynski of the California Governor's Office of Planning and Research (OPR) put me in touch with the right people and supplied important documents as well as trenchant commentary. Ray Brubaker and Jack Jones at Dow were very open and cooperative—if I ever wanted someone to build a clean, environmentally sound plant for me, I'd call Ray Brubaker—as were local officials like Richard Brann of Solano County. Bill Press, a major actor in the Dow case as head of OPR, and Larry King and Clement Shute, both formerly with the California Attorney General's Office, were equally accessible, and the kind of people one likes to count as friends, gracious men of good mind and good humor. Michael Storper, now a professor at UCLA, was another indispensable source, not only of facts but of critical analysis, and Leslie Emmington of Berkeley introduced me to the people of Collinsville and their lore.

Looking back at the help I received from these individuals and scores of others makes me recall what Joan Didion wrote in a preface to one of her books. She worried that in telling a story she might somehow betray the honesty and openness that her probings met with. You will meet many good people in these pages to whom, I hope, I have been faithful.

Christopher J. Duerksen
October 1982

Chapter 1

CALIFORNIA MEANS BUSINESS

For years California was in the forefront of the environmental movement in the United States. Governor Jerry Brown preached about an "era of limits," "small is beautiful," and "the three-gallon flush." He abolished the state Department of Commerce, which promoted economic development, and opened an Office of Appropriate Technology. The Golden State was home of the nation's first and most comprehensive coastal zone protection law, an environmental impact reporting system that made the National Environmental Policy Act (NEPA) look puny by comparison. California also had local growth control plans so stringent that towns like Livermore and Petaluma gained national and even international prominence. That all changed in 1977. Jerry Brown was suddenly courting business and industry with unabashed zeal both at home and abroad. He even sported a "California Means Business" button on his lapel. As columnist David Broder observed, "Brown started acting like his old man, not the apostle of the new spirit." Why?

The Fantus Company, a Dun and Bradstreet subsidiary that helps firms select sites for plants, warehouses, and office buildings, published a study in 1975 of state business climates based, among other things, on labor costs, business taxes, and legislative climate. It ranked California next to last. That had something to do with Brown's changing spots. A 1976 unemployment rate of 9.4 percent—above the national average of 7.6 percent—was undoubtedly another factor.

At first, nothing much changed in California. Jerry Brown will tell you that he rarely reacts dramatically to such things: "I postpone them for further reflection." Brown, as he told his biographer Orville Schell, likes to use a crisis as a take-off point to find solutions to broader issues. And the crisis was soon in coming.

In January 1977, Dow Chemical Company announced that because of environmental and regulatory roadblocks it was cancelling

1

plans to build a huge 13-plant, $500 million chemical complex on the banks of the Sacramento River northeast of San Francisco. That decision sent shock waves up and down the state. Labor leaders, with an eye on the dismal unemployment figures, were livid at the thought of losing the 1,000 construction and 1,000 manufacturing full-time jobs the Dow project promised. Business leaders began passing the word across the country that it was "ABC" when it came to building plans—"Anywhere But California." Brown could not revive Dow's plans, but the stage was set for him to do something about the growing conflict between industry and environment in his state, to show the business community that he was not all that bad, to put a little distance between himself and an increasingly embattled environmentalist constituency.

The mood in California was changing once again. Two decades ago it had been rampant growth, then an anti-growth attitude in the early 1970s. Now there was ambivalence. In the 1960s, California was synonymous with growth. It eclipsed New York as the most populous state in 1962, and its annual population increase peaked at a staggering 600,000 people in 1963. The state had almost tripled its population in only 30 years. Growth was good, something to be proud of, prosperity for the construction and development industry, for the finance, transportation, and service sectors. In San Francisco a big electric billboard flashed the good news as it toted up a burgeoning population. Growth was something to be accommodated, not questioned.

Jerry Brown's father, governor of California from 1959 to 1967, made his mark by doing many of those things that his son would later come to stand against. Pat Brown pushed through the largest bond issue in U.S. history to finance a grandiose plan to bring water from the wet north to the dry south. At the ground breaking for that project he boasted, "We are going to build a river 500 miles long" in order "to correct an accident of people and geography." No "era of limits" then.

By the mid-1960s, however, a reaction to all this growth set in. The environmental crisis, later to assume national proportions, was already brewing in California. Yosemite National Park was so full of people, tents, clotheslines, and smoke on weekends that it resembled a shanty town. Los Angeles vanished in a cloud of smog on bad days. Hardly anyone wanted to know the way to San Jose any more, so marred was the journey with housing and commercial development.

The fires of environmental revolt were further stoked by an oil leak from a Union Oil Company well that smeared the beaches of Santa Barbara and the collision of two Standard Oil tankers just outside the Golden Gate. For days television newscasts treated Californians to close-ups of oil-covered waterfowl dying wretched deaths. Books with titles such as *How to Kill a Golden State*, *The Destruction of California*, and *The California Revolution* chronicled the devastation. According to one commentator of the day, "To become a conservationist in California, all you have to do is look around you."

The San Francisco Bay Area, where Dow would make its ill-fated effort to build, was at the forefront in the environmental revolution. It was the scene of one of the earliest revolts against highways—citizens confronted planners and traffic engineers by opposing and stopping first the Embarcadero Freeway and then one that would have sliced through Golden Gate Park. Another campaign was waged against the filling of San Francisco Bay, which had been reduced to 60 percent of its original size by local governments and developers who wanted more cheap land for housing, industry, and garbage dumps. The result was establishment of the Bay Conservation and Development Commission with broad authority to protect this great natural resource. Scores of environmental groups were spawned during this period, including Friends of the Earth; others, such as the Sierra Club, added legions of new members.

By the early 1970s the brakes were being slammed on growth all over the state. The California Environmental Quality Act, enacted in 1970, required an environmental impact report to be filed for most government projects and approvals, including the issuance of permits to developers. A statewide referendum in 1972 established a coastal zone regulation scheme that would serve as a model for similar controls in other states.

But at the same time there was a countercurrent, little noticed at first, one that would surface in the Dow case. It began in 1969 as President Nixon cut back on federal spending. He hurt his home state most of all, strangling its defense and aerospace industry. A slowing economy attracted fewer people—natural population growth soon exceeded net migration—but it also failed to create enough new jobs for a labor force that continued to expand at a rate 36 percent higher than that of the nation as a whole. The situation was exacerbated by the national recession of 1973-1975, just as the Dow project was made public. The stage was set for a monumental clash between environment and industry.

Thus, once again California seemed to be anticipating the rest of the country. *Newsweek* asserted in 1974 that "California is where everything good or bad, trivial or important, seems to happen first in America." It had led the nation's environmental revolution. Now, it would be the first state to face squarely the multifacted envirobusiness conflict that would sweep the country in the late 1970s— jobs versus clean air and water; the tension between seemingly endless project environmental reviews and the need to understand the consequences of growth; the delay and uncertainty faced by industrialists as they tried to escape what they perceived as an environmental permit maze juxtaposed against carefully crafted laws designed to protect against known environmental hazards. Jerry Brown characterized the conflict as "a chess game with very few moves." The Dow case and California's reaction to it would set the stage for a national debate on the subject.

Of course, what happens in California is not necessarily a pole star for the rest of the nation. As native daughter Joan Didion observed, the truth about the place is elusive and must be tracked with caution.[1] California is different, in many ways a country unto itself. If independent, California would rank seventh among the world's economies, ahead of Great Britain, Italy, Spain, and Brazil. It has more land than England and West Germany combined, and a huge and enticing market for industry (with around 22 million people, California is the most urbanized state in the country) no matter what the environmental rules it must play by. Perhaps California can afford to be a bit more aloof to business than other states.

Yet, there is no denying we all love to imitate or hate California. Somehow it seems that what happens in California is often repeated elsewhere. Or, if California stumbles, the rest of us chortle and congratulate ourselves that it won't happen here. Either way, we apparently learn. Thus, as *Forbes* magazine counseled in an article that appeared the same month that Dow dropped its expansion plans, business and political leaders would be wise to follow closely the envirobusiness conflict in California because it seems likely that one day they'll be singing California's new tune, whatever it turns out to be. Environmentalists might want to heed that advice, too.

Chapter 2

DOW IN THE DELTA

What exactly was Dow Chemical Company planning for California and the Sacramento River Delta? After months of preparation and behind-the-scenes talks with federal, state, and local officials, Dow announced in February 1975 that it would construct a 13-unit, $500 million petrochemical complex 35 miles northeast of San Francisco. Half would be built on 600 acres of a 2,700-acre parcel on the banks of the Sacramento River in the windswept Montezuma Hills of Solano County. The rest would be built in the industrial town of Pittsburg, California, half a mile away across the river on a 250-acre site in Contra Costa County, where Dow had operated another facility producing chlorine, caustic soda, and other chemicals since 1940. If all went well, Dow planned to start construction in 1976, have the first plant producing by 1978, and finish the whole complex by 1982. (Maps, photographs, and a chart appear between pages 66 and 67.)

The new facility would use salt, plentiful in the Bay Area, and 40,000 barrels a day of naptha, a distillate of crude oil similar to kerosene that is produced by local refineries as a by-product in making high octane low-lead fuel. It would convert them into substances like acetone, ethylene, styrene, and vinyl chloride—the basic building blocks for hundreds of everyday products. Dow planned to sell some of these chemicals directly to other manufacturers for use in making goods ranging from boats and car bodies to styrofoam cups, kidney dialysis filters, and paints. Ethylene and propylene would be piped under the river in gaseous form for further processing in Pittsburg. This would be the first major petrochemical facility west of the Rocky Mountains, with a capacity to supply 40 percent of the raw materials needed by West Coast plastics manufacturers.

To build this facility, Dow would need a minimum of 65 permits from a host of federal, state, regional, and local agencies—dredge and fill permits from the U.S. Corps of Engineers, air and water pollution permits from state and regional agencies, easements and leases for use of state land, and local building and land-use permits.

5

DOW PETROCHEMICAL PROJECT
SUMMARY OF PERMITS REQUIRED

	Purpose	Number Required	Total
FEDERAL			
U.S. Corps of Engineers	(a) Dock and ship turning basin	1	1
	(b) Water intake	1	1
	(c) Water discharge	1	1
	(d) Pipeline crossing	1	1
U.S. Coast Guard	(a) Transport (operational) over dock	1	<u>1</u>
Subtotal (Federal)			5
STATE			
Regional Water Board	(a) NPDES for osmosis reject	1*	1*
	(b) NPDES for water return on dredging spoils	1	1
	(c) Certificate of conformance	1	1
	(d) Evaporation ponds	1 ea. pond	2**
	(e) Sanitary treatment (even if no discharge)	1	1
	(f) Storm water run-off from land maintained in ag use	1	1
Water Resources Control Board	(a) Appropriative water rights	1	1
Dept. of Water Resources	(a) Dam safety	1	1
Fish and Game	(a) Alteration of stream bed for dock, water intake, and pipelines	1 ea.	3
Reclamation Board	(a) Alter levees	1	1
State Lands Commission	(a) Lease for easements across state lands for dock, pipelines, and water intake	1	1

	Purpose	Number Required	Total
Bay Area Air Pollution Control District	(a) Construction	1 ea. plant	13***
	(b) Operation	1 ea. plant	13***
Subtotal (California)			40

COUNTIES

	Purpose	Number Required	Total
Sacramento	(a) Use permit for pipelines	1	1
Solano	(a) Building	1 ea. plant	7
	(b) Sanitary	1	1
	(c) Potable water	1	1
	(d) Grading	1	1
	(e) Use permit for pipelines	1	1
Contra Costa	(a) Building	1 ea. plant	6
	(b) Grading	1	1
	(c) Use permit for pipelines	1	1
Subtotal (Counties)			20
GRAND TOTAL			65

*   Obtained September 26, 1975.
**   Absolute minimum number of ponds is two.
***Absolute minimum since each plant has at least one vent. The styrene plant alone would have required 14 permits.

This list of permits was compiled by Dow Chemical Company.

In addition, formal environmental impact analyses were required under both federal and state law.

Why had Dow chosen this spot on the Sacramento River for its huge project? Why hadn't all those permits and California's reputation as a state willing to enforce its environmental laws scared it off? To find out, I drove out north of San Francisco to Dow's Western Division headquarters in Walnut Creek to talk with Jack Jones, one of the few remaining company officials still around the area in 1979 who took part in the Dow battle. Jones had been part of the original project team, personally responsible for getting those 65 permits.

The name Walnut Creek conjures up visions of a quiet place in the country, but as with so many places in California, the name is history and the reality is something less. Only 30 years ago it was a small town in the midst of great walnut groves that gave the community its name. The walnut trees are mostly gone today, replaced by a middle-class suburb with a population of 49,704. Walnut Creek has its own BART stop and is home to a growing number of corporate offices.

Dow moved its Western Division headquarters here in 1976 from blue-collar Pittsburg, a few miles to the north, joining its research department that had moved 14 years earlier. The Dow labs had already won an architectural award in 1966 from the city. The place is pleasant, with low-rise office buildings, well-tended lawns, and all sorts of greenery. Pleasant, but not too showy, and above all, efficient. The only thing that disturbed me was the groundsman who was sweeping the walks clear of leaves and dust with a gas-powered blower—I had just spent an hour in line trying to buy gas for my rental car. I shrugged that off as purely California. (Then, six months later, I saw one being used on the sidewalks of Washington, D.C.)

Dow is proud of these quarters. This same proud attitude, sometimes bordering on arrogant, permeates everything Dow does. Dow is particularly proud of its environmental record—and not without reason. As the environmental movement gained momentum in the late 1960s, Julius Johnson, the firm's respected director of research, persuaded top officials to tackle the company's environmental problems head-on. Johnson argued that not only could Dow be a good citizen, but that it could make a profit at it. Carl Gerstacker, then Chairman of Dow, threw his weight behind Johnson and a truly revolutionary program was born. As one Dow official told me, "We decided not to fight the pollution thing, but to make money at it."

Dow made money by recovering valuable chemicals from waste effluents and by energy conservation. At its Corning plant in Michigan, a $2.7-million investment to recover chlorine and hydrogen from air emissions associated with silicone production saved the company $900,000 per year in operating costs. It was one of the first firms to discover cogeneration, for example, using waste heat from one process as an ingredient in another. The Western Division was active, too. It had won many awards for taking its Pittsburg plant "off the river"; that is, instead of dumping wastes into the Sacramento, it recycled chemicals from the effluent. These are only a few of many such examples.

Organizational changes were also made within the corporation. Pollution control responsibility was devolved to each major plant, where ecology councils were set up to oversee implementation of environmental guidelines established at corporate headquarters in Midland. Pollution control performance was made a factor in evaluating the performance of plant managers. This isn't to say Dow completely escaped pollution control problems. In Ohio it was charged with mercury pollution of Lake Erie and in Canada it paid $450,000 in damages for dumping mercury into the St. Clair River. Start-up problems with a chlorine plant in Stade, West Germany, led to chlorine gas emissions that outraged local citizens. More recently Dow has been sued by the U.S. Environmental Protection Agency (EPA) over air pollution from its Midland, Michigan, facilities. But other chemical companies had just as serious if not worse pollution problems; all in all, at least at this time, Dow was proudly at the forefront of corporate environmental initiatives. It urged its approach on other chemical companies.

Dow's pride can be seen, too, in small things like flowers and shrubs around its plant in Pittsburg—a stark contrast to the slovenly, half-hearted housekeeping of its industrial neighbors such as U.S. Steel and Continental Can. But this pride sometimes makes Dow belligerent when challenged or criticized.

Until 1965, Dow was hardly a household word. Saran Wrap was its biggest consumer product. But then the company decided to produce napalm for the Vietnam war. Napalm or liquid fire was responsible for the grisly scenes the nation witnessed almost daily on the evening news—villages burning and children running down roads, their clothing seared off and skin charred. War protesters began to focus on Dow. There were marches on Dow plants in Torrance, California, where napalm was produced. Company re- cruiters were harassed on visits to college campuses.

But Dow was undaunted. Instead of backing off as many companies would have done, Dow fought back. In a 1968 *Business Week* article, Dow President Ted Doan summed up the company's feelings:

> We deliberately confront the issue in our recruiting. It is necessary as a matter of principle. One never knows how far he will go in standing on principle until confronted with a specific issue, but we feel we should be able to talk to these kids. This way you're not a hypocrite. One of the student complaints about business now is that it doesn't stand for much except profits. Maybe we ought to take a stand or two for the benefit of the kids . . . .[2]

Dow kept making napalm until 1969 when it lost out to a lower bid from another company.

Dow was just as contentious when EPA announced its intention in 1979 to partially ban use of 2,4,5-T (an herbicide that made up half of Agent Orange, used as a defoliant in Vietnam) in the United

States because the agency suspected it was unavoidably contaminated with a deadly dioxin. Hundreds of Vietnam veterans have
claimed compensation for a wide range of illnesses they allege
resulted from their exposure to Agent Orange. EPA, alarmed by
the high rate of miscarriages among women exposed to 2,4,5-T,
wanted to stop its use as a weed killer on forests and highway rights-
of-way, while still permitting it on pastures and rice paddies.

Almost alone, Dow fought EPA, arguing that 2,4,5-T was safe
and that there was no concrete evidence to the contrary. Its zealous
defense of the product sometimes degenerated into personal attacks
against critics like Barry Commoner. Dow also fought with producers of several television specials on the use of 2,4,5-T. According
to the *Los Angeles Times*, Dow's public affairs manager Gary Jones
wrote a letter of complaint following the airing of ''A Plague on
Our Children,'' a highly controversial public television documentary. When he got a reply he didn't like, Jones stamped the letter
with an expletive and sent it back to the show's producer.[3]

The company continues to fight EPA on a range of environmental
standards. As one company official told me, ''It doesn't make sense
to clean up that last 5 percent of pollution. The cost isn't worth
it.'' That uncompromising, ''I'd rather fight than switch'' attitude
would play a role here. Zolton Merszei, former president of Dow,
was quite gruff when asked by a journalist in 1976 about environmentalists or governments that might block his development plans.
''Unless we are really wanted, to hell with them. There are plenty
of investment opportunities in the world.''

Knowing that reputation for feistiness, I was a little surprised
that Jack Jones and others at Dow were so cooperative. True, it had
taken a little time to clear corporate channels, but Jones and his
associates really did want, it appeared to me, to do what they could
to improve the siting process and to learn the positive lessons of
the bitter fight they had been swept up in. In my efforts to reconstruct
the details of the controversy, only one Dow official, Al Look, who
headed the Western Division in 1974 and now runs the Dowicil
Division in Texas, refused to speak to me. Look alleged that I was
focusing too much on the problems associated with the project
instead of on its benefits.

Jones, like many of Dow's people, is from the Southwest, an
Oklahoman who doesn't look like he ought to be in a governmental
relations slot, but rather out in the field honchoing a big project or
bellying up to a local bar on Friday with the boys at quitting time.
Jack dealt with state and local agencies. He worked long and hard to

build the big facility and, people say, has some bitter feelings towards some of the state officials who questioned Dow's project planning. But the animosity, if there, doesn't show. He speaks in an even, almost quiet tone, picking his words carefully as if he has gone over all of this many times in his mind. "We chose this site simply because it made most sense from a business point of view," Jones says. "The market was already there—we'd simply produce on the West Coast what we were already producing in Texas and Louisiana and save $60 million in transportation costs. There were no major suppliers on the West Coast so we could cut costs and capture a bigger share of a growing market."[4] Dow's experts predicted, in fact, that by producing in the heart of the market the firm could capture 40 percent of all demand for plastic feedstocks west of the Rockies. And consumers would benefit too. A study by the Stanford Research Institute estimated the costs of shipping materials from east of the Rockies raised prices to West Coast consumers by 6 percent.

This strategy made Dow the most highly profitable chemical producer in the world by 1975, leaving other U.S. companies such as DuPont and Monsanto in the dust. Its return on equity in 1974 was a stunning 28 percent! If Dow saw an opportunity to capture a market, the company moved quickly to build a new plant, be it in California, Brazil, Yugoslavia, or Korea. The central office in Midland, Michigan, coordinated investment policies, but the various divisions spread around the world, each with its own president and headquarters, were given near autonomy to develop and execute building plans. Thus, once capital for the project was allocated by Midland, the Western Division—one of the entities making up Dow U.S.A., one of six Dow divisions—had a free hand in getting the big facility built.

There were reasons, too, for choosing a site in Solano County. It was close to Dow's Pittsburg plant, "a known quantity," according to Jones, with 800 employees and proved technical capacity available to help build the new facility. But why didn't Dow just build the whole thing at the existing Pittsburg site? Everyone knows it's easier to do that than build from scratch—less problem with existing neighbors than with new ones and fewer worries about meeting a different set of environmental and land-use regulations.

Jones agreed and said Dow had tried to do just that. But even though Dow had 400 acres at its Pittsburg plant, almost enough to squeeze the new facility onto, Dow wanted a buffer zone or greenbelt around its new plant to give it some breathing room and to protect it from complaints by its neighbors. Jones claims that Dow negotiated with

U.S. Steel to buy an additional 400 acres of land that company owned next to the Pittsburg site, but that U.S. Steel refused to sell because it wanted to reserve the land for expansion. "We'd have been nuts to have put half the plant across the river if we could have expanded at Pittsburg." Critics respond that it was a half-hearted attempt by Dow and that the company wanted more land around its plant so it could exploit a loophole it had found in the Clean Air Act.

Although it is hard to pin down the truth seven years later, U.S. Steel officials do say that in 1974 and 1975 the firm probably wouldn't have sold because of favorable market prospects for steel at the time. Also, Jones has correspondence showing that Dow entered into negotiations with U.S. Steel. He claims that Dow actually suspended project planning for a time in 1974 when it appeared the sale might go through.

The Solano site was also a natural from a transportation perspective. Being on the Sacramento River, it offered one of the last accessible deepwater moorings on the West Coast capable of docking ocean-sized tankers, a key factor for any chemical plant dealing with huge tonnages of raw material. All that Dow needed to do was dredge a basin near the shore to allow ships to turn and maneuver. A railway line was also nearby.

Jones added that as West Coast oil refineries started producing more unleaded fuel in the 1970s, "we were going to have naptha coming out of our ears." Naptha cannot easily be upgraded to gasoline without serious environmental problems, particularly nitrous oxide emissions. Thus, Jones says, local refineries saw a chance to relieve this problem by selling naptha to Dow.

Wouldn't this somehow be tied in with Alaskan oil? Not so, Jones claimed, but in 1975 *Chemical Week* magazine quoted Earle Barnes, then president of Dow U.S.A., saying that "the complex was conceived to utilize oil and gas that will be coming from the Alaska North Slope."[5] Dow's planners apparently believed that Alaskan oil, when added to increased production in California, which has major oil reserves, would lead to a surplus of crude on the West Coast in the late 1970s (an accurate assumption, it turns out), which would mean relatively cheap fuel supplies. Secure feedstocks are critical to Dow because, unlike many of its competitors, the company lacks access to its own oil or gas. But Jones maintains that the economics of the plant did not hinge on cheap Alaskan oil. "Naptha could be purchased on the open market or shipped from Texas."

The economic and business reasons for building a chemical complex in Solano County did, no doubt, make a lot of sense. While environmental groups would later argue that the ease with which Dow could handle an unsophisticated rural county government played a major role in deciding to locate in Solano County, even hardcore critics of the project, such as Michael Storper of Friends of the Earth, agree that "from a strictly business point of view, Dow had every reason to choose that location."[6] In organizing to build the Solano County complex, Jones explained that Dow formed a project team of four people: "Al Gunkler was the chief engineer, Beckee Beemer took care of the environmental aspects, Bob Perry was the paper man, and I was in charge of getting permits."[7] The team also included Dow's local attorney, Art Shelton. Because of Dow's policy of divisional autonomy, this project team was largely on its own with little guidance from the environmental experts or legal talent based at corporate headquarters in Midland, Michigan. However, according to Jones, "We weren't scared by the number of permits needed. Most were routine, and we are a big company with experience in dealing with such matters." But in some ways, the Western Division was new to the development game, particularly when it came to building a big facility from scratch.

The Western Division is an odd duck in the Dow family. Dow is often called a chemical company's chemical company because it produces basic feedstocks that are sold to other manufacturers who produce intermediate products or finished goods. It got its start in 1897 when a young chemist, Herbert Dow, found a way to extract chlorine, sodium, and bromide from saltwater beds that underlie a large area around Midland, Michigan. The family-run company prospered and by the 1970s trailed only Dupont and Monsanto among the country's chemical giants. Aside from Saran Wrap, however, Dow didn't produce many products familiar to the average consumer and was not much known until it decided to produce napalm.

But the Western Division was never a major petrochemical producer. Bearing the name Great Western Electro-Chemical Company, it was purchased by Dow in 1938, the firm's first major expansion outside Midland. Originally, production centered around caustic soda and carbon tetrachloride; even today, caustic soda, a necessary reagent in many manufacturing processes, is the "bread and butter" commodity of the Western Division. But the Western Division also produces many "end" products now: pesticides, specialty chemicals, a range of plastics, including polystyrene, styrofoam, and even some familiar consumer items such as Dow-Gard bathroom cleaner. The Division also has a large, highly respected research arm. Facilities are scattered in several cities throughout California, but

Pittsburg is the mother plant. While these plants have been continually modernized and expanded, the Western Division has not built a major new facility in many years.

Neither Jones nor others in the Western Division believe that this seeming lack of experience hampered Dow in adequately evaluating possible adverse environmental and land-use impacts associated with the Solano County site. But was it a good site from an environmental and land-use point of view? And what of the alternatives? Some environmentalists like Storper point out that the project environmental impact statement prepared by Dow's consultant devoted only four pages to discussion of alternatives (such as Los Angeles, nearby Avon, California, and the state of Washington)—and even then two of the pages were devoted to the Solano County site and design alternatives there.

Moreover, environmentalists claim that Dow didn't do its environmental homework on the Solano County site, failing to take into account, among other things, air quality problems in the area, lack of proper zoning, and possible damage to the nearby Suisun Marsh. (The largest contiguous wetland in California, the Suisun Marsh serves as a principal wintering ground for migratory birds on the Pacific Flyway.) One state official offered a more subtle criticism. He said that Dow didn't really have any high-powered people involved, no one with an ability to say "yes" or "no." "They were public relations types. We didn't ever understand who the man in charge really was. They never had a full-time man in charge of this siting only. Somebody high up should be in charge, a full-time man. Not a PR man."

Jones disputes the charge that Dow didn't do its homework. He says that Dow met throughout 1974 with representatives of the Bay Area Air Pollution Control District (BAAPCD) who assured them that the area was not then and would not be classified a non-attainment area—one that failed to meet national ambient air quality standards established by the Clean Air Act, an air quality designation that would make any new construction exceedingly difficult. Dow also talked with local county officials, who told them that the land-use plan for the area called for industrial development on the site, and even with representatives of such environmental groups as the Sierra Club and the Planning and Conservation League (PCL's then director, Bill Press, later would be deeply involved in the dispute as head of the California Office of Planning and Research).

Jones claims that the environmentalists felt "quite comfortable" with the project, considering it a local rather than statewide issue.

"Terrain was a problem, but we could design around the hills which would fence the plant off from public view," Jones says. "And air quality wasn't supposed to be a problem. We almost went elsewhere because of uncertainty over water supply and quality [Dow would use as much water as a city with 40,000 people]. That's a big issue here, but we figured we could handle that."

On this basis and, claims Jones, with assurances from the state that the project would be given a high priority, Dow announced its plans formally in February 1975. Characteristically, Dow plunged into the process with great impatience. It purchased a short-term option on the 2,700-acre Solano site and then, when the county gave a preliminary go-ahead, plunked down $6 million to buy it rather than taking out a long-term option contingent upon final project approval, as most prudent developers do in this era of increasing uncertainty in the siting process.

Dow told the various agencies involved that it was beginning work on the necessary state and federal environmental impact analyses and expected to start construction in only 280 days, even though it often takes that long in California to secure necessary permits for a small residential development. Jones says Dow had to hurry because it needed West Coast capacity by 1982 when its Texas plant would be fully committed to supplying other areas. Ray Brubaker, who would later be called to the rescue when the project bogged down, adds that time means money. "When Dow decides to get into a project," he said, "it's always smart to build it as quickly as possible, especially with a high inflation rate." Again, probably smart from a strictly business point of view, but the seeds of conflict were being sown.

Chapter 3

SOLANO COUNTY AND THE HILLS OF MONTEZUMA

"Can a Quiet Agricultural County on the Sacramento River Find True Happiness with a Huge Messy Chemical Plant?" That was the title of an article about the project written by local environmentalists that appeared in a Friends of the Earth national newsletter. Environmentalists like to paint Solano County as a rural backwater on the banks of the Sacramento that was simply too unsophisticated to cope with major industrial development. Supporters of the project draw a different picture. While conceding that the county was largely agricultural, they argued it was no country bumpkin. It had a rapidly growing population and a major industrial center long established in its eastern half. In any case, they pointed out, Solano was heavily influenced by the major manufacturing complex just across the river in Pittsburg and Contra Costa County.

After spending several days traveling around Contra Costa and Solano Counties, visiting the main towns and talking with people, I would say each camp is about half right. While there is still a farming tempo about life in many of the area's small towns—somnolent summers and winters, hectic late springs and falls—the place is far different from the quiet Kansas wheat-growing country where I was raised. The very name of Pittsburg, home to Dow, U.S. Steel, and scores of other heavy industrial producers, gives a clue to the area's other character. But the place is no Los Angeles either. It is still possible for factory workers to rush home from work, pick up a fishing rod, and be out on a deserted pond or river bank for a few hours of casting before dark.

Pittsburg was laid out in the mid-1800s by a young William Tecumseh Sherman, who envisioned a metropolis on this site so well served by the wide Sacramento River. He called it the New York of the Pacific. During the gold rush the town was a busy port, but things soon quieted down. Salmon, sturgeon, and striped bass fishing became the economic backbone of the area. Not until the early 1900s did heavy industry begin moving to the town, which then changed its name, appropriately enough, to Pittsburg.

Today, the entire south bank of the Sacramento in Contra Costa County, from its confluence with the San Joaquin River downstream twenty miles to the river bridge over the Straits of Carquinez, is a collage of smokestacks, power lines, oil storage tanks, and the other accoutrements of big industry. Things don't change, either, on the Solano County side of the bridge in Vallejo and Benicia. Both of these towns, with a combined population of about 85,000, are heavily working class. Many commute across the river to work in the factories of Contra Costa County. Both have large populations—over 25 percent—of blacks, Latinos, and Asians. Benicia is known for its large port and distribution complex and an Exxon refinery built during the 1970s. Vallejo is home to a huge naval shipyard at Mare Island which employs 15,000 people. Countywide, twenty times as many people work in non-agricultural jobs than agricultural ones. The military employs one of every 10 residents, most at the naval shipyard at Mare Island and at Travis Air Force Base near Fairfield. Not exactly idyllic farm country.

But outside of Benicia and Vallejo, northwest on Interstate 80, which runs through the county seat of Fairfield west to Sacramento, the scenery changes dramatically. Factories and warehouses give way to farms and orchards. Silhouettes of a mothballed naval fleet fade into the marshes of Suisun Bay. The rich and fertile farmland in the eastern part of Solano County produces important cash crops such as tomatoes and sugar beets. The transformation is complete in the western half of the county in the Montezuma Hills, whose steep, rolling, wheat and sheep country overlooks the river and Pittsburg on the far shore.

All in all, agriculture pumped almost $110 million into the local economy in 1974. This is the "sleepy" Solano County that environmentalists portray. With its wide, flat valley flanked by tall hills, the place could be the setting for a Hollywood cowboy movie. The hills are a tawny brown with only a few lone oaks here and there—a great place for riding into the sunset.

Ironically, this graceful landscape is largely man-made, transformed into something far different from what it once was. Early travelers across the Suisun Valley rode through wild oats so tall that riders on horseback were sometimes hidden. They sometimes stampeded the plentiful elk and pronghorn. But the oats don't grow and the elk don't roam anymore. The proud Suisune Indians, an independent and self-reliant people who once ruled all this land, are gone too, but not without a fight. Some of the tribe, instead of giving in to Spanish invaders after one bloody battle, set fire to their huts and perished in the flames. American pioneers would later finish the job.

The Suisune have left behind only their name—the Suisun Marsh—and that of their great chief, Solano. Solano was overlord of all the Indian tribes north of the Suisun and San Pablo bays. The land where Dow wanted to build, and much more, was once his. Baptized as Francisco Solano by the fathers of Mission San Francisco de Solano at Sonoma, he later became a strong and faithful ally and close friend of Lieutenant Mariano Vallejo in the 1840s. When Solano County was organized in 1850, it was named at Vallejo's request for his friend. "A splendid figure of a man," as Vallejo described this 6'7" giant, "he was a keen, clearheaded thinker, readily grasped new ideas, learned to speak Spanish and was so ready to debate that few cared to engage with him in a contest of wits."

Farms and orchards many years ago replaced the natives here. Even the last physical evidence of their presence—a statue erected to honor Chief Solano—was shot up by local yahoos. Today, instead of wild oats, it is sugar beets, pears, field corn, wheat, and tomatoes. The infamous square California tomato is king, the county's leading crop. Canneries and grain mills are important employers. Yet even here change is in the air again. Just outside of Fairfield a new Anheuser-Busch brewery has taken a chunk out of a large pear orchard, lured by a county government intent on attracting more jobs and securing a bigger tax base. Beer amidst the blossoms.

A once-important commercial fishing industry based on the Sacramento River has been decimated by pollution, overfishing, and intrusion of saltwater as more and more freshwater has been diverted from the Sacramento and San Joaquin Rivers upstream for irrigation and drinking water. So rich were these fishing grounds at the turn of the century that large fishing fleets had worked out of Solano County ports such as Collinsville and Benicia. A young Jack London worked here and later wrote of the times in his *Tales of the Fish Patrol*: "The waters of the bay contain all manner of fish, wherefore its surface is ploughed by the keels of all manner of fishing boats manned by all manner of fishermen."[8] Oldtimers claim that they could walk across the smaller rivers on the backs of spawning salmon. Chinook salmon still migrate annually through the Bay and Delta, but in greatly reduced numbers. Commercial fishermen take

about 500,000 annually, but Solano County gets little direct economic benefit from this activity. Today, about the only commercial
evidence of this river bounty is a small crayfish processing operation
employing two people.

The politics of Solano County are as diverse as its landscape.
This used to be solid Republican country in the 1950s, but as its
population grew and the military invaded the area, the political face
of Solano County changed. The farm areas stayed Republican, but
the Democrats gained strength and today hold a 3-2 majority on the
county board. That's not to say this is Jerry Brown country—you'll
find few ardent admirers of the governor here.

Although Solano County has the second smallest population among
the nine counties in the Bay Area, it has been one of the fastest
growing since 1970. People have come in search of cheap housing
(in short supply in the Bay Area, some claim, because of no-growth
environmentalists).[9] In fact, so many new houses have been built
in places like Suisun City, which has almost tripled its population
of 3,000 since 1970, that state and county officials worry there won't
be enough tax revenue to pay for needed municipal services. Overall,
population grew about 10 percent between 1970 and 1975, and another
10 percent by 1978. While the number of jobs has not quite kept
pace with this population surge, Solano County has done much
better than the rest of California.

But if Solano County was already growing, perhaps too rapidly,
and attracting jobs, why then the courtship of Dow? Quite simply,
say county officials, it was not clear in 1975 whether the population
growth would continue or if there was a sufficient tax base to pay for
the new residential construction already under way. Local governments
in California were among the first in the country to realize that new
residential construction rarely pays its way; that is, property taxes paid
by new home owners do not cover the cost of new roads, sewers,
water, and other services that local governments must provide.

Solano officials felt particularly vulnerable since the county's
largest employer, the military, paid no property taxes. The Dow
facility would have added almost $5.6 million per year in property
taxes to Solano County and 14 percent to its total property tax rolls,
assuming all 13 units were built, and would do so without bringing
in too many new residents who would demand services. With a
jump in local unemployment during 1975 from 5.9 percent to 6.7
percent, county officials were even less certain that there would be
enough jobs to go around. It was in this context that the county's
small industrial development agency went into high gear. The red

carpet was rolled out for industry with little debate whether Solano
County, with its tiny, 12-person planning department and no specific
controls or land-use guidelines for the massive industrial park envisioned in its plans for the Collinsville-Montezuma Hills area, could
handle additional growth.

Today, county officials like Richard Brann, chairman of the five
member county board in 1975-76, grudgingly admit to mistakes. Brann,
vilified by some environmentalists during the Dow dispute as a thought-
less pro-growther, is a big farmer from Rio Vista, a typical rural
representative—honest, sincere, a somewhat conservative Republican
hostile to too much government interference with growth, yet edgy
that his way of life won't survive the changes he supports. Brann is
pleased that one local reporter said he neither looks nor acts like a
politician. And he doesn't—the doubleknit sportcoat and wide tie he
wore when we met didn't quite fit the big farmer's hands and country
accent. Brann's family, like those of all his fellow board members,
at least up to the last election, goes back several generations in Solano
County. Brann defends his actions.

> Up until 1970 there was a free-wheeling, pro-growth atmosphere. Many
> residential developers came in then and bought land. They could get it
> cheap then. They're still developing ground they bought and annexed
> in the very early 1970s. It nearly got away from us. The brewery just
> got put in the wrong place. I despair every time I go along I-80 and see
> it sitting out there where there used to be pear trees. But it's in the
> city—a cherry-stem annexation. We've slowed down the annexations
> and growth now. A couple of city councils have a strong no-growth
> attitude. We have a strong county policy now that all growth must take
> place in urban areas, so now we've got 95 percent of the population
> living in cities.

Brann also maintains that the county's attitude towards industrial
development, while a very positive one, has been responsible.

> We tried to locate industry in industrial parks or near a city. But the
> area down by Collinsville is a unique resource, an entirely different
> situation. Because we have tended to promote that, we're branded as
> gung-ho industry who want to bring in the smokestacks and pollute the
> country and do nothing but turn the county over to big industry. But
> this isn't the situation at all. I think we're trying hard to have a responsible
> plan so that we can get on top of it and have whatever comes in be a
> credit to the county. Certainly we were looking for Dow to help the tax
> base of the county, but that wasn't our overriding objective. It's the
> only deepwater area left on the Pacific Coast. National Steel purchased
> the MacDougald property over 15 years ago—that focused attention on

the area—and then PG&E [Pacific Gas and Electric] bought their property. That committed the area to ultimate development.

Brann's rather fatalistic view of how planning for an area works
(landowner expectations determining ultimate use) would be scored
by many environmentalists and land-use planners, but, like it or
not, landowner expectations are a powerful, often dominant force
in land use planning.[10] Thus, when Collinsville landowners began
promoting the area as prime industrial property in the 1960s, a force
was set in motion that, when not countered in its early stages, became
increasingly difficult to harness. The farmland was sitting there as
picturesque as ever, but its future was already being etched in stone.

Environmentalists and land-use planners would also differ with
Brann's rather rosy view of Solano County's planning capabilities
and successes. Some say Solano can't wait to be Los Angeles. The
State of California stripped the county of its primary planning authority over the Suisun Marsh in 1974 and vested it with the more
conservation-oriented Bay Area Conservation and Development
Commission (BCDC). Brann claims it was just a power play by the
state. He says that the county was doing a good job preserving the
marsh, but records show that it had been greatly reduced in size
and that development continued to nibble at its edges. The county
zoning map still designated part of the wetland for industrial development in 1979, but BCDC rules, which take precedence, pre-
clude any building there. Also, while the county has a 160-acre
minimum for most farms and more than 60 percent of its land under
Williamson Act contracts, which give tax breaks to owners who
agree to keep their property in open space and farmland, the county
started worrying about saving farmland only recently. Further, it
has not been shy in cancelling Williamson Act contracts when
potential developers came forward.

In the Montezuma Hills, however, where Dow planned to build,
most of the Williamson Act contracts are still in force. That makes
for a striking transition as you travel from Fairfield and Travis Air
Force Base on its outskirts into the hills—big jumbo jets to weathered
redwood barns and four-lane highways to narrow, dusty back roads,
all in the space of a few miles. The Dow environmental impact
statement calls this gently rolling country, but to a flatlander like
me the hills seem steep. The consultant who wrote "gently rolling"
probably never sat in a tractor tilted precariously on those hills
working a field. So upright and rounded, they resemble beehives,
especially just after circular contour discing gives them a ridged

look. There is remarkably little development on the hilltops. Most of the farm buildings and houses are nestled in pockets at lower elevations to avoid the wind. Only a few gas wells, electric powerline towers, and big old oaks break the undulating horizon, the area's most striking feature.

Dow officials always refer to the Montezuma Hills as marginal farmland, which gets up the dander of local folk who love it here. The Stan Andersons are typical of the farm families in the area. Four generations of Andersons have tended 2,000 acres, a large chunk of it rented from Pacific Gas & Electric (PG&E), alternating wheat and barley crops with sheep grazing and fallow on a three-year cycle. Dow points to the fact that the average yield here in a good year is only 20 bushels per acre (compared with 35-40 bushels per acre on good Midwest farmland).

But the Andersons are good farmers who know how to care for their land. They use no fertilizers and do not irrigate their land. There are no gullies on the steep hills, in contrast to farm country in many parts of the South and Midwest. The pastures are not overgrazed. The margins of fields are carefully disced in the summer to help contain any fires that might sweep the area.

"This has always been like our land," says Mrs. Anderson. "We've always treated it like our own. It really makes me boil when I hear people make gross statements about this land. If anything, I feel guilty about the bounty it has given us in the past." Still, it isn't what the agriculture experts call prime farmland. The soil isn't especially fertile and the rainfall is spotty (13 inches per year) so it takes a lot of acres to support one family even modestly. There are only 61 farms in the 50,000 acres that make up the hills.

The Andersons live comfortably but modestly; they have no air conditioning to fend off the scorching summer sun, although a small swimming pool helps. Stan Anderson is the typical quiet farmer. He doesn't say much unless something important is on his mind. His wife, who fought Dow and then a nuclear power plant proposed by PG&E, does most of the talking. She's a thoughtful, plain-speaking lady. Despite her efforts against Dow, she's no strident environmentalist. No conspiracy theories here; no deep-seated animosities. She even says that Dick Brann is an honest and bright man. "He's just industry-minded, but thinks he's truly doing right. Unfortunately the whole county is about 20 years behind in its thinking about growth."

Mrs. Anderson was one of the most eloquent speakers at the state hearings on the Dow project, asking penetrating questions in an honest, forthright way. Yet, today she feels frustrated. "What can you say about these big projects? The average person doesn't have the background to challenge what they tell you. They like to locate in remote areas like this where there are only a few people to watch them. We went to meetings year after year on Dow and the PG&E nuclear plant and all the others. It got so we couldn't farm. They just wear you down. I'm exhausted now—just hope somebody else will come in."

While the Andersons stood to lose part of their farmland to the Dow and other industrial projects planned for the area, people in nearby Collinsville had even more at stake. The town would be effectively surrounded if the area was developed as envisioned by Solano County. While the Dow plant itself would be a few miles upstream and would not directly affect Collinsville, other industries and PG&E had their own plans. Some say it would not be much of a loss if Collinsville, a hamlet of a dozen or so ramshackle houses and only four families, was obliterated.

Collinsville, hard on the banks of the Sacramento, has a unique claim to fame. It is perhaps the only surviving town in the United States built on stilts. Collinsville's access to deep water made it an important stopover for steamers plying the river between Sacramento and San Francisco Bay in the 1880s. Some picked up grain from surrounding farms and others refueled. At the turn of the century it was not unusual to see 20 riverboats a day dock there.

Fishing was also good here, especially for salmon and sturgeon, drawing many Italians from Genoa and Naples. They maintained a semi-friendly running battle with fish patrolmen like Jack London. "To protect the fish from this motley floating population many wise laws have been passed, and there is a fish patrol to see that these laws are enforced," London later wrote. "Exciting times are the lot of the fish patrol . . . ." The Italians built the houses on stilts alongside the river. Besides allowing the fishermen to row their boats right up to their front doors, the stilts protected the houses from periodic flooding. With all this activity, Collinsville prospered, boasting by 1920 a hotel, a movie theatre, a cannery, shops, two churches, and a school.

Today little is left. A fire in the 1920s burned much of the town and the fishing industry collapsed when California put tough restrictions on commercial salmon netting in the 1930s. But Joe Vitale, who has lived here all his life, says that things were going bad before then.

In the 1920s we could drink this water, but then they dug the ship channel. The saltwater came in and the ships going up and down the river spoiled everything. The sand piled up and we couldn't even get close to our houses by boat anymore. My father was born here in the 1890s and I've lived here for all my life. It was a good fishing village.

Joe, still active and far younger-looking than his 64 years, has hung on here with his feisty wife Billie, a former WAC sergeant, by catching the odd fish off the jerry-built docks that still stand on the water's edge and by taking care of the local cemetery for the county. Billie and Joe live in a house separated from the river by a grass-covered dike. Small and a little broken-down on the outside, inside the house is neat as a pin. Billie, a diminutive outsider who came here to marry Joe, rails about the big corporations she says are doing the area in. Joe is quiet, somewhat fatalistic about what's going on, but obviously proud of Collinsville and its history. He made me stay for a beer so we would have time to go through the file of newspaper clippings and photographs he dug out to show me. Joe was not deeply involved in the fight against Dow. In fact, the only real opposition in Collinsville came from Bill and Leslie Emmington, brother and sister, who own 15 of the 27 acres that compose the town proper.

Bill, a public school teacher, describes himself, only half-facetiously, as one of the twenty-five environmentalists in the county. Leslie works for a historic preservation group in Berkeley, where she lives. Three generations of Emmingtons have called the area home. Their grandfather was a Swedish immigrant who changed his name from Johannson and bought land at Collinsville. His son, their father, owned and ran a hotel there in the early 1920s, when the area was still relatively remote and wild, but Bill's mother, a city girl, could not cope with the hard life there and the Emmingtons eventually moved away, ending up in Berkeley. The hotel was taken over by squatters and finally burned.

All the Emmingtons have left here is a small parcel of land on the river, most of it marshy or overgrown with weeds. Silty brown water, a constant wind, and big power plants and industry just across the river—not a very appealing place, even for an environmentalist. The Emmingtons tried to interest a sailing club in using the area as a marina, but no dice. They tried to give it away to The Nature Conservancy, but their offer was rejected. According to Leslie, the Conservancy said the site looked good for industrial development.

However, only a stone's throw to the west of the Emmingtons' property, Montezuma Slough, the eastern border of the Suisun Marsh, empties into the Sacramento. Because its conditions are ideal for opossum shrimp, the slough is one of the Bay Area's main nurseries for striped bass, who eat the little crustaceans. Striped bass are an important sport fish in the Bay Area and Delta. They spawn here and spend the first summers of their lives within a few miles of the confluence of the Sacramento and San Joaquin Rivers.

The Suisun Marsh, the place where the salt water from the Pacific Ocean and the fresh water of the Sacramento and San Joaquin Rivers meet and mingle, is even more important to geese and ducks. When I first heard people talking about the Suisun Marsh and its waterfowl, visions of the Chesapeake Bay duck marshes danced in my head. The Delta has even been called the "Everglades of the West." But I found something completely different. Suisun Marsh is what the biologists call a highly managed wetland. You can actually drive out into the marsh's 85,000 acres to see how water levels in various sections are controlled by a series of dikes and small flood gates. By raising and lowering water levels, refuge managers try to assure that the maximum amount of food and a suitable habitat will be available to the hundreds of thousands of ducks, geese, and other waterfowl that use the marsh, particularly in winter.

Historically, California's Central Valley was covered with large expanses of grassland interspersed with freshwater marshes and broad floodplains. At mid-valley, the Sacramento and San Joaquin Rivers joined to form a delta. There were 5 million acres of sloughs, wetlands, and meandering waterways in California in 1850, about 460,000 acres along the coast. The Suisun Marsh was prime habitat for tremendous flights of migratory waterfowl along the Pacific Flyway. Ducks and geese that summered in Canada and Alaska came through here on their way south, and many stayed for the winter.

But in the Central Valley, as elsewhere in the country, agriculture and people had a greater call on the land. Beginning in the 1950s reclamation began; wetlands were drained, dams built, water sucked up for irrigation. Today, only 140,000 acres of wetlands remain along the coast. The Suisun is the biggest surviving marsh, a mainstay of waterfowl habitat in central California. Further, it has international as well as national importance: 60 percent of the waterfowl in the Pacific Flyway winter in the Central Valley.

Therein is the rub. Unlike ducks and geese in the Central Flyway, whose well-being hinges on limited nesting areas in the northern U.S. and Canadian prairie provinces, waterfowl in the Pacific Flyway have larger quality breeding grounds in Alaska, western Canada, and the Aleutian Islands. On the other hand, waterfowl in the Central Flyway have plenty of wintering ground in the relatively undeveloped, rural central United States, but waterfowl on the Pacific Flyway aren't so lucky. So refuge managers believe that if anything happens to Suisun Marsh and the few other remaining wintering grounds in California, the results could be devastating.

Like most wetlands, the Suisun Marsh doesn't bowl you over with its beauty. You've got to get down into it to really appreciate what's there, and even then it's not easy. "The strong winds make fishing a bitch," a retired factory worker told me, as he heaved out his big bait rig into what felt like a gale. But, still, I saw dozens of fishermen hunkered down along the dikes waiting for the tap-tap of a channel cat or maybe even a black bass or crappie. There are a lot of birdwatchers out here, too, especially in the fall and winter. In the jargon of statisticians, there are 115,000 man-days of recreational use in the marsh, 75,000 for fishing, bird watching, motor boating, and hiking, and the rest for hunting. Fifteen thousand of those man-days are spent on 50,000 acres owned by private duck clubs, whose members are mostly wealthy outsiders. Two private duck clubs own land farther up the Montezuma Slough above the Emmington's land.

To the east of the Emmingtons is a small "resort" called the Collinsville Marina. Resort really isn't the right word—it is more of a river rat's den where weekend campers can park their rigs, drink beer, and catch a few fish. In fact, rumor has it that the place stays open only because the county winks at the flagrant health and sanitary code violations there.

Bill and Leslie will tell you that, aside from Joe Vitale, they really are not close to the families left behind in Collinsville. They only occasionally visit their land and are watched warily by the locals when they do. Leslie remembers seeing the Italians working clandestinely to repair their nets when she was a girl—commercial net fishing was banned by the state in 1957 anywhere upstream of the Carquinez Straits.

But netting goes on today, almost a habit passed on from father to son, and modern-day fish patrollers have their hands full. The poaching isn't small-time, either. The state caught one fish dealer who had purchased more than 100,000 pounds of illegal fish in one five-year period during the 1970s. Leslie knows the locals now poach beaver and muskrat on their land and illegally fish from the Emmington's dock.

So there was an uneasiness in the air when Leslie, pale-skinned and red haired, picked her way carefully along the Emmington's decrepit dock to stand chatting with the dark, young Italian boys who had several lines in the water and a few fish on their stringers. They tried to act nonchalant, but each was watching her every move out of the corner of one eye. Leslie spoke in her quiet voice, trying to draw them out, but they answered only with a word or two. These Italians keep to themselves.

Some environmentalists who fought Dow say it was no accident that the company chose this area around Collinsville to build in—only 235 people, and clannish ones at that. In fact, Bill Emmington, the Andersons, and a few other dedicated local environmentalists were forced to wage a lonely local campaign. Ironically, they succeeded in stopping Dow, but were worn out in the process and are now unable and unwilling to fight PG&E, National Steel, Atlantic Richfield, and the other companies that have lined up to develop the site now that Dow has run interference for them.

Bill Emmington is pained by what he sees as Collinsville's future. "Collinsville and the land around will be drastically transformed if all the development plans come off." PG&E was first in line with a proposal to construct a coal-fired power plant—a 1,600-megawatt facility. The utility has had its eye on Collinsville for many years. It proposed a nuclear power plant here in the 1950s. That effort was thwarted, but PG&E held on to its land. In the wake of Dow and with a serious oil shortage facing the country, PG&E came back touting coal. State officials, on record against nuclear power, initially reacted favorably, but falling energy demand has helped shelve the project, at least temporarily.

PG&E is hardly alone. National Steel and Southern Pacific Railway own more than 1,300 acres here just west of Bill's land. Atlantic Richfield Polymers, a subsidiary of ARCO, proposed a billion-dollar petrochemical plant a few miles to the east in 1976.

In the face of it all, the Solano County board remains confident it can keep industrial development "out of the hills," mitigate adverse environmental impacts, and handle any secondary growth impacts. Maybe, but one thing for certain is that Collinsville as it has existed the last 100 years will be no more. Already, say Joe Vitale and Bill Emmington, the county is working to squeeze out the last small landowners. Joe has been told that the county won't pay him any longer to keep up the little cemetery, which means he'll have a hard time making ends meet. Bill claims that since the land is being zoned industrial and for commercial recreation, he may be forced to sell off to meet increased property taxes. Goodbye, Collinsville.

Chapter 4

THE OPPOSITION MOUNTS

After announcing its project in February 1975, Dow plowed ahead to get the necessary permits and approvals from the state of California and Solano County. Except for permits needed to use river water, a critical commodity in this region, and the environmental impact review required by the California Environmental Quality Act, the state agency approvals were relatively minor. Most were easements and leases to lay pipelines across state-owned property. Local approval was the key—rezoning from agricultural to industrial use, cancellation of an agricultural land preservation designation, and an environmental impact report (EIR) required by state law. Dow would stumble each step of the way.

Dow bought its land for this project from a farmer named McOmie (no one ever referred to him except by his last name), who had moved to Solano County from the southern part of the state where he had been run out of farming by developers. Of course he made a pile of money in the process. His neighbors, who didn't know him well, say he was a little strange, keeping to himself in a big house on his ranch.

For years before Dow purchased the McOmie Ranch, the property had been zoned for agricultural use. Although the county's comprehensive land-use plan, which established guiding principles for growth and land-use control in the area, was somewhat ambiguous, it was clear, at least to opponents, that the county did not contemplate conversion of the McOmie property for another decade. While land downstream around Collinsville was designated for future industrial development, the McOmie parcel was just outside this area. Further, the plan's language indicated that the area should remain agricultural.

Environmentalists jumped on this discrepancy. They argued that to satisfy California zoning law, which requires that all zoning be in accord with an applicable comprehensive plan, Dow should have first sought an amendment to Solano County's comprehensive plan redesignating its property for industrial development. After that had been accomplished, Dow could then have petitioned the county to rezone the property. This process may seem a bit roundabout, but many other states require a similar procedure, the idea being that before a particular piece of land is rezoned, the local authority should consider how the change will affect the area's overall growth picture. If rezoning deviates from the policies set forth in the comprehensive plan, it should be rejected or the plan amended first. As Larry Silver, a Sierra Club attorney, told me, "From a strictly legal point of view, the county plan was really screwed up, and we had a good argument that it did not contemplate manufacturing, at least of this magnitude, in the area."

At the state hearings convened later to consider the project, Art Shelton, Dow's local attorney, argued this was just a minor quibble.

> As a matter of fact, the southeastern general plan for Solano County did have all the requisite elements in it, and there is nothing in this world that is more clear than that band along the river for water-oriented industry. The only reason it's chicken hatch markings in the book of the general plan is because some professional planners don't like to draw lines because people say, "Hey, it's not on that side of the line or that side of the line." And that isn't good for a general plan because it's supposed to be kind of flexible. So they use things that look like the footprints of chickens. And they dot them around the map. And now somebody says, "If they're not inside that chicken footprint, why that isn't supposed to be industrial."

Whatever the case, Dow exposed its flank by having the property rezoned from agricultural to industrial without first changing the comprehensive plan, an action that would have been a cinch given the county's support for the project. Jack Jones blames Shelton for being asleep. Some environmentalists claim Dow simply thought it could steamroll the rezoning through, since the county was sympathetic.

But rezoning was just the first step. Not only was the Dow property zoned for agriculture, it had what is called a Williamson Act contract on it. In the 1960s the California legislature, worried that rampant development throughout the state was eroding its agricultural land base, the state's largest industry, enacted the Williamson Act.[11] A few years after it was passed, the Williamson Act was amended to allow protection of recreational and open-space land and wildlife habitats. Instead of relying on zoning controls to protect farmland

and open space, the act provides significant local property tax breaks, subsidized by the state treasury, to landowners who sign a contract with the appropriate local jurisdiction agreeing to forego any incompatible development. The contract, which stays in force for a minimum of 10 years and is enforceable in court, can be broken only if the local authority makes specific findings set out in the act itself. The landowner is also required to pay a cancellation penalty reflecting the value of the tax abatements already received.

In 1970, Mr. McOmie voluntarily entered into a Williamson Act contract with Solano County, agreeing to forego any nonagricultural use of his land. By contracting not to develop his 2,700-acre ranch, only 300 acres of which were prime agricultural land, McOmie saved himself several thousand dollars a year in taxes. He renewed the contract automatically over the next four years by not requesting that it be cancelled, so that when Dow purchased the land, the contract was effective into the 1980s unless the county agreed to cancel it.

At this time, a good deal of Solano County farmland was under Williamson Act contracts. In fact, 50 percent of the county's land was in agricultural preserves by 1978. Statewide, more than 11 million acres were under Williamson Act contracts by 1973; only 12,595 had been cancelled,[12] a small bit of this in Solano County. Dow needed to cancel the contract on only about 1,300 of the 2,700 acres, since more than half the parcel would remain in agriculture as a buffer zone.

The state law gave local governments a good deal of discretion in drafting Williamson Act contracts, but they could be terminated prematurely only if, in the lawyerly words of the statute, "the cancellation is not inconsistent with the purposes" of the law, "cancellation is in the public interest," and there is "no proximate, noncontracted land suitable for the use to which it is proposed the contracted land be put." None of the cancellations around the state had been subject to serious legal challenge up to 1975, and there was no case law regarding the findings required upon cancellation or the meaning of clauses like "not inconsistent with the purposes" of the law and "no proximate, noncontracted land." Larry Silver says:

> This was a state law question of great magnitude. There had been relatively few cancellations, so that's why people got very freaked out. During the first four years of the act's existence, the acreage taken out of contracts was less than what Dow wanted to take out. If it was going to be that easy for Dow to cancel a Williamson Act agreement just

because a landowner wanted industrial development on his property, then it was clear there was very little protection for agricultural land in the state. Conservation people had thought that the contracts were binding and that they couldn't just be cancelled.

Dow's Jack Jones concedes that the company did not fully comprehend the political context in which such a major cancellation would take place, but pleads that Dow's local counsel did not understand that the Williamson Act was geared to protect open space as well as farmland, thus making cancellation more difficult to justify. Jones says, "We knew about the contract, but didn't anticipate cancellation problems. You know a contract's not forever. So we paid way too much for the land—$2,800 an acre. We really got ripped off."

At the state hearings, Art Shelton maintained he knew exactly what was going on.

Somebody stood up here and said, "Well, there haven't been but a few cancellations for the first few years of the Williamson Act." Well, of course, there wasn't. Farmers were just putting it in, and in the first few years it was restricted to prime land. And they weren't taking it out. Lately a lot has been taken out . . . . There's a whole chapter in the Act that's devoted to taking it out, and there is a whole section telling how you compute the fee and everything. We paid almost a quarter of a million dollars to take that property out. That sort of thing has to be there if you are going to have any kind of flexibility whatsoever. I happened to have served on a planning commission for five years when the Williamson Act contracts were being entered into. I have attended planning commission conferences and I can tell you on the local level that all commissioners understood that was a contract that could be bought out. So people entering into it and the members of the Board of Commissioners signing it all understood that those things were cancellable.

Dow had a third obstacle to overcome. Before Solano County could approve Dow's project, the California Environmental Quality Act—called "seequa" for its acronym, CEQA—required that an EIR be prepared. Most of the early CEQA disputes were over residential developments, the kind of growth that was having such a visible impact on the countryside and environment statewide. The Dow project, more complex by far in the permits it would need and its environmental impact, would be one of the first major industrial developments to be reviewed under CEQA.

CEQA had been patterned after the National Environmental Policy Act (NEPA), which requires a similar report for federally approved projects. But in many respects CEQA was more demanding. If a more environmentally acceptable alternative site was available, there had to be good reasons for not choosing it. NEPA only requires an agency to consider, not adopt, such alternatives. Moreover, CEQA was originally conceived to apply only to projects in which the state or a local government had a direct role, or at least that's what many industry people thought. But at the urging of environmental groups and the state attorney general's crack team of environmental lawyers, the California Supreme Court held that it applied to any project with a significant environmental impact that required a permit from a state agency or local government.

Solano County took the lead in drafting the EIR because it was most directly involved with the project, even though the county had only a small, already overburdened staff of just 12 people in its planning office. This might not have been a problem if the county had simply hired an outside consultant to prepare the report for it, with Dow footing the bill.

But Solano committed an incredible blunder: it allowed Dow to contract directly with a private firm to write the document. Although it was not an uncommon practice throughout California and the rest of the country for a developer to pay for an environmental impact analysis and to have a say in who will write it, Solano should have handled it differently. Dow could have prepared an informational draft that Solano would have reviewed, analyzed, and judged independently; or the county could have contracted with a consultant, who would then have owed allegiance to the county, not Dow. California courts have specifically approved of such an approach.

Despite the fact that the consulting firm hired by Dow, J.E. Gilbert & Associates, was well-respected, the county and Dow would be haunted with the appearance of impropriety throughout the planning process. As one environmentalist later commented, "Dow's local lawyer didn't appear to know better, but Jerry Gilbert should have. They carefully plotted their own destruction."

Despite these serious self-erected hurdles, the county and Dow pressed ahead. Notices of the rezoning and Williamson Act contract cancellation were published and work on the EIR began. No red flags went up to warn them of the problems ahead. Local environmentalists had not been watching the project closely and statewide organizations based in San Francisco, such as Friends of the Earth and the Sierra Club, did not appreciate that other industries were lining up behind Dow to develop the area.

Almost simultaneously, however, two developments changed the

climate for the project. First, Cynthia Kay, a local environmentalist
from nearby Vallejo who was on the county's zoning mailing list,
received notice of the proposed reclassification of the property from
agricultural to industrial use.

> I raised the issue at a joint meeting of the Northern and Southern Cal-
> ifornia Conservation Committee of the Sierra Club in the spring of 1975.
> I went down to the meeting in Monterey and made a presentation. After
> that the Sierra Club organized a North Bay Task Force and we started
> watching the project. Then I packed up and went on vacation, and by
> the time I got back there was a whole variety of new faces concerned
> about Dow. At the first county meeting I went to when I got home, I
> met Nick Arguimbau, Michael Storper, and Barbara Des Rochers, who
> all straggled in from Berkeley. That day we had a meeting at my parents'
> house in Fairfield, and started talking strategy and setting up lines of
> communication.

Kay, Arguimbau, and Storper would form the backbone of the
opposition to Dow. A more unlikely trio is hard to imagine. Kay
is in her 30s, the oldest of the three. She is a pretty lady, small
with graying hair, and big brown eyes conveying a real honesty
and sincerity. She lives in a modest house in Vallejo with her
husband, a Navy photographer. Kay speaks slowly at a very measured pace as if testing the sound of each word before releasing it.
She questioned the need for the new plant and its products, but says
she never set out with the idea of stopping it. Unlike some others,
she sees no evil conspiracies at the local or state levels to grease
the approval of the Dow project.

Arguimbau is also small, not much bigger than Kay. He is almost
elfin in appearance, with thick glasses and big ears, a lawyer who
came out of law school in 1975 to work for the Environmental
Defense Fund and with Larry Silver of the Sierra Club on the Dow
case. Arguimbau is suspicious of many people's motives in the Dow
controversy, talking about questionable contributions to politicians
and political monkeying at the local level. He comes across as a
real rock-ribbed environmentalist, someone you wouldn't like to
lock horns with in court. He's tough and likes to fight. Some of
his opponents apparently don't like Nick—the night before we met,
an arsonist torched his firm's office.

Storper, on the other hand, is tall and handsome, a geographer
at the University of California at Berkeley, very bright and well-
spoken. Storper comes across as less combative than Arguimbau,
but his soft-spoken, thoughtful manner cannot disguise his strong

environmentalist leanings. Storper would do most of the organizing and fund raising to keep the Dow opposition going.

The efforts of this trio were spurred by a second event. Soon after Dow made its plans public, Atlantic Richfield Company (ARCO) announced that it intended to build a "world scale" chemical complex just upstream from the Dow complex. Dow and others maintain ARCO really had no intention of building anything at all and that the whole thing was a ploy either, depending on whom you talk to, to keep up with a competitor or to catalyze local opposition to a big industrial complex.

One thing is for certain, it got environmentalists worrying, in Storper's words, "that we'd have another Ruhr Valley or Houston Ship Channel. The Dow plant was going to be a turning point for Solano County environmentally, economically, and socially." Storper would later write that:

> The possibility of a major industrial complex rivaling some areas of the eastern United States makes one shudder. Solid industry along both banks of the Sacramento River, vast increases in shipping, and pollution deadly to fragile Suisun Marsh. Large residential communities in now-rural areas. Higher taxes to pay for the problems that are inherent in urbanization—higher crime rates, environmental deterioration, increased demand for social services. These problems are supposedly the "price" we must pay for economic security, for more goods, and services.[13]

In a workmanlike fashion Kay, Arguimbau, and Storper monitored the project's progress. They attended zoning board meetings, the debates over cancellation of the Williamson Act contract, and the nine public hearings the county held to consider the EIR. And they became increasingly disenchanted with what they heard and saw.

They viewed the draft EIR, prepared in a near-record time of six months, as grossly inadequate on several key points. Kay complains that the EIR contained very little information to answer questions raised at the hearings. "Dow simply wouldn't come up with some of the technical information on air quality and the hazards of running pipelines across the river." Further, she charges that the Dow people were very hard to talk to and that the county simply did not respond to regional, state, and national interests. She adds that:

> Alaska and the glut of oil on the West Coast was the key issue and the county couldn't deal with it. It was outrageous to me [that] they were the lead agency on a project like Dow. The planning of Collinsville should be just set aside as a national resource. If you look at the land-

holders there and the proposed use, it's either major energy production
or use. All uses of a national concern. It was well beyond the ability
of Solano County to plan and deal with this.

Storper adds that the EIR really didn't consider alternative sites
as required. In his view, Dow had already made its decision based
on business factors. "Look at the EIR. Less than a page was devoted
to alternatives in Washington and other areas in California." But,
in Dow's defense, it should be recognized that the sophistication
of environmental impact statements throughout the country in dealing with alternatives was, at the time, marginal at best. Environmental impact analysis was still in its infancy, with the real struggle
being to get agencies to adequately evaluate the major impacts of
a project, not what the alternatives might be. Thus, no matter what
the law said, few environmental impact statements dealt with alternatives. That would come later, after the courts made clear that
CEQA and NEPA required more than just a passing glance at adverse
environmental impacts.

Environmentalists also worried about air pollution, the impact of
potential oil and chemical spills on Suisun Marsh, the seeming
indifference to secondary growth Dow would spur and its costs,
and the huge amounts of water Dow would withdraw from the
Sacramento River. They raised a host of subsidiary issues: the
advisability of building a plant and running pipelines across the river
in an area criss-crossed with major earthquake faults, Dow's plans
for disposing of toxic wastes produced by the facility, and the
potential pollution from the significant amount of power the Dow
complex would require.

Air pollution is a big issue in California, not only in Los Angeles
but also in San Francisco and surrounding counties. The Bay Area
has bad air that fails to meet federal standards for dust and smoke
particles, for smog-causing hydrocarbons produced in the burning
of coal and oil. Pollution from cars is also bad at times. At high
levels, none of these pollutants is good for your lungs nor for plants
and crops, not to mention the fact that nobody likes to have soot
on his car or windowsill.

While air pollution permits could be issued only by the Bay Area
Air Pollution Control District (BAAPCD), the EIR was supposed
to give everyone an idea of how significant emissions from the Dow
complex might be and where the wind might carry them. Environmentalists were particularly concerned that prevailing winds might
blow the pollution into the Central Valley, California's agricultural
cornucopia, and adversely affect crop production. Some claimed

there was already evidence that pollution from the Bay Area was affecting tree growth in Yosemite National Park, hundreds of miles away. They also dramatized the fact that emissions from a lead smelter at nearby Selby had been linked to the deaths of horses that had eaten contaminated grass on area ranches. (The smelter was closed in 1972.) To top things off, a state official estimated that agricultural losses due to pollution in California amounted to $55 million in 1974.

The level of air emissions from the complex projected by the EIR set off alarm bells. Dow predicted the plant would emit 8 tons of sulfur dioxide and 2.5 tons of hydrocarbons a day, both figures high enough to raise serious questions about whether the project should be approved. To add to these concerns, some sharp-eyed people actually took time to read the EIR in detail and discovered that the Dow complex would emit an organic chemical called chloroethylene.

To most people, chloroethylene doesn't connote anything bad, but it is a lesser-known synonym for vinyl chloride—an essential ingredient in many plastic gizmos we use every day. Vinyl chloride had been making headlines around the world at the time: several workers in several different countries had died of a rare liver cancer linked to vinyl chloride exposure. To make matters worse, environmentalists obtained data from the Texas Air Quality Board that showed that a Dow chemical plant in that state emitted a whopping 16.3 tons of vinyl chloride a day.

Dow's project coordinator, Bob Perry, argued that those figures were out-of-date and that emissions from the new plant would amount to "a drop in the ocean."[14] Jack Jones added that "the proposed facility could have been put inside the Texas plant and you couldn't even find it. It was only a quarter that size and Texas produces a lot of other things." Even though the Solano plant would be cleaner and despite the fact Dow had a commendable record in protecting its workers from exposure to vinyl chloride, following more stringent guidelines than legally required, the unfortunate use of the term chloroethylene and Dow's refusal to say how much vinyl chloride might be produced made it appear as if the company was trying to hide something.

Another key issue that worried environmentalists was the prospect that an oil or chemical spill from the project would wash into the Suisun Marsh. Already reclamation, agriculture, and industrial development had shrunk this critical wildlife habitat from 750,000 to 85,000 acres.

Could it survive with a massive industrial complex just upstream? What would happen to the million or so birds that visited the marsh each year if an oil tanker cracked up in the treacherous currents of the Straits of Carquinez that had once almost claimed the life of Jack London? Could the wildlife of Sherman Island, which sits in the middle of the river with a long, exposed shoreline, survive? What hazards would an almost 100 percent increase in tanker traffic (from 180 ships per year on the lower Sacramento River to 345) bring with it, especially since the area was sometimes enshrouded in thick fogs? And what if a ship ran into the chemical-laden pipes running across the river bottom or if an earthquake fractured them?

Dow countered by pointing to its virtually spotless oil-spill record, but Michael Storper wasn't persuaded: "Other planned industrial facilities (e.g., an ARCO plant) would increase the number of ships moving up and down the river, too, leaving a past history of no spills a flimsy solution to a real hazard."[15]

I pressed Storper on the earthquake—was it really that serious? Storper said it wasn't inconceivable. About 10 minutes later, as if to convince a doubter from Kansas where the land hasn't moved for a long time, a temblor measuring 6.5 on the Richter scale rippled through the Bay Area. Storper dove underneath his kitchen table as I contemplated, wide-eyed, the large rubber plant swaying wildly in the next room. Dow would later produce a detailed spill control plan, but its failure to address the issues adequately at the outset gave the opposition added ammunition.

Water was another major issue that emerged early. It is a particularly precious commodity in California. More than 40 percent of the state's natural runoff runs into the Delta. Much is used for irrigation; 30 percent is exported to farmers in the San Joaquin Valley and to southern California. Dow needed to pump water out of the Sacramento River and then desalinate it for use in plant processes. Some of this water would be returned to the river, but the average net consumption would be 4,000 gallons per minute. The practical effect, according to the EIR, was that saltwater would intrude 200 or 300 feet farther up the river than before.

Environmentalists worried that this intrusion would further damage the wetlands in the area and the fish and wildlife that frequent them. They also charged that the water would in effect be "stolen" from upstream agricultural uses, highly dependent on irrigation, since more freshwater would have to be released from dams and canals to keep saltwater from intruding into low-lying farm areas. If freshwater flows weren't increased, farms in the Delta would be adversely affected unless other users cut down to make up for Dow's withdrawal. The EIR recognized these problems and although it suggested methods to mitigate adverse effects, the problems were dismissed as "insignificant and largely theoretical."

These were all serious problems in the eyes of opponents, but secondary growth—the new county residents and houses they would require, local government services, and downstream industries—that Dow might induce probably bothered the San Francisco-Berkeley contingent as much as anything. Californians are extremely sensitive to the costs associated with new development, particularly residential. By the early 1970s many California cities realized that new residential growth did not pay for the services demanded unless the houses were expensive and the owners paid a lot of property taxes. Their reaction was to cut down on high-density developments and to require developers to build schools or pay money in return for approval of their plans.

Today, with the aid of state and regional planners, many localities use sophisticated computer models to determine whether a development will pay its way. But some of the cities in Solano County had a bad record. Kay says that the Association of Bay Area Governments (ABAG) recently cautioned Suisun City that it would be bankrupt in 10 years if it continued approving so much new housing. Suisun's response? According to Kay it was, "We figure more like three years." That attitude worried people.

The opposition questioned whether the complex would really pay for itself. True, they conceded, Dow would bring in a lot of tax revenue, but had anyone at the county calculated how much it would cost to service the complex with new roads or sewers? They pointed out that the county had no detailed development plan for the Collinsville area that would help estimate such costs and indicate who might bear them. Opponents also made a telling point that Solano County was hard pressed to answer. Most of the tax revenue from the facility would go to the county while the burden of providing services for Dow employees would fall to the cities where they would live. And there was no mechanism under state law to share this revenue.

Storper, in particular, worried that even if the tax revenue from Dow could somehow be used to pay such costs and take care of services demanded by any new residents, the industries that followed Dow or were attracted by its presence might overwhelm the county's financial resources. Cynthia Kay had harsh words for the Solano County Industrial Development Agency: "The county was so eager for industry at the time it was just falling over itself. The county had a strong industrial development agency that was kissy-kiss with Dow. They just groveled all over.''

Michael Storper echoes Kay, criticizing the county for what he says was its unthinking boosterism. "Solano County is a prime example of public subsidy for private industry. Secondary costs are never discussed in the EIRs. It's the reason taxes rise (strangely) after the developers move in. Public finances have been managed toward dependence on an endless cycle of industrial growth and commercial expansion. The county is up for sale; its price is below cost.''[16]

Environmentalists weren't very confident either that Solano County would keep secondary industrial and residential growth away from the Suisun Marsh or out of the Montezuma Hills. While I could see why they might worry about the hills, which were under county jurisdiction, wouldn't the more environmentally oriented Bay Conservation and Development Commission (BCDC) protect the marsh with the help of the Suisun Resource Conservation District? It had a pot of money to acquire a buffer zone around the marsh. The BCDC had been vested with land-use power over the marsh in 1974. If the BCDC did not like a development, it could refuse to approve it even if Solano County wanted the development. And this was true with respect not only to the marsh, but a large buffer zone around it too.

But, according to project opponents, things looked better on paper than in practice. The BCDC had not yet completed its marsh protection plan and was thus operating on an ad hoc basis. No one could be certain that the plan or the buffer zone, which existed only on an interim basis, would be approved by the state legislature, as required by law, or that either would stand up in court.

Dow admitted in the EIR that some "downstream" plants would be attracted by the complex given the availability of raw materials from the new plant, but maintained that most growth would take place in Contra Costa County and would in any case pay its own way. Dow also pointed to a report it had commissioned by Stanford Research Institute (now SRI International) that showed an overall net benefit to the county from the development's multiplier effect. Every dollar that the company and its employees spent would generate more business and thus revenue for the county.

Storper counters that neither the SRI report nor the EIR touched on the overall impact of ARCO, PG&E, National Steel, and other industries that might join the parade to Solano. But, as one Dow official would later point out at a public hearing, evaluating the impact of these other potential industries was nearly impossible.

> Our problem is that we really don't know what to say about other companies' future plans for a piece of land which that company owns. This would be for PG&E, Southern Pacific, National Steel, or Atlantic Richfield. And I wonder if you want to see such a thing in the EIR or in the information that we put out to justify or to help work out the problems in our project. If you could make some suggestions on what you would like to see or what your recommendations would be for us in addressing ourselves to the growth inducement that might come about in Solano County or in Contra Costa County, it may or may not have an impact. It depends on what these other companies choose to do. We are no more privy to information on any one of these than anyone else. You read the morning paper, and that's what we do, also.
>
> As Jack [Jones] mentioned, Atlantic Richfield is a competitor, and they don't tell us what processes they use, what products they tend to make or would make in such a place. It makes it very difficult for us to come up with any reasonable description of growth-inducing impact for companies which not only are not under our control; they really don't talk to us.

Dow and Solano County also defend the early EIR hearing process and the document that emerged from it, and do so just as vigorously as the environmentalists criticize it. Dow officials point to the 200 plus-page EIR and to the scads of hearings they had to attend. One consultant to the project told me that he could understand why environmentalists might have been less than thrilled with the hearings. "It wasn't that they didn't have a chance to comment, but that they had to appear in an unfriendly forum—the counties were in favor of the project." "Anyway," Jack Jones points out, "most of the objectors were outsiders."

Clayne Munk, tall, slow-moving, soft-spoken, and amiable head of the Solano County Planning Department, agrees. "We were engrossed in things intensively for about two years. We held meetings and a lot of them. There was a lot of publicity from the *San Francisco Chronicle* and the *Sacramento Bee* to our local newspapers. Nothing was hidden. And still we only had about five protestors."

As to charges that the EIR consultant worked for Dow, Munk simply responds, "I can truthfully say that they were under our control. They made hundreds of changes at our direction. But at the early stages the money did go directly from Dow to the consultant. Now it's funneled through the county after the consultants bid on a job.''

Munk does concede that his small planning staff was hard-pressed to deal with the complexities of the Dow project, but maintains that the analysis was adequate. "We only had eight people when I came here in 1974 and 10 or 12 during the project. Two were assigned to Dow. But we did have a lot of help from Contra Costa County's Planning Department, which was a lot bigger and more sophisticated. State agencies also participated. The whole process went on for many, many months. I thought we did a thorough job.''

Munk is particularly irked by claims that the EIR's analysis of the project's social and economic impacts on Solano County was not complete.

> This was one of our [the county planning department's] areas. We had to consult and rewrite this section at least twice. It does take care of that point. We started on the premise that we wouldn't have another city or urban sprawl out there. This type of development facilitates mass movement of people in and out because they can regulate their shifts. If we just let people out there it would destroy the agricultural area and marsh so we had to guard against that. The construction period would bring in a lot of people, but after that the operation would have been quite modest. Primary residential is the drain on county resources. Most of the industries that would come in here have their own resources, their own fire protection, water, and sewer, and their own police guard so the county would basically provide backup and maintenance of primary access roads.

But it isn't clear from the original EIR that the county really understood exactly what this industrial development would cost. The EIR did recognize that any new residential growth would require added sewage treatment capacity, but no cost estimates were given. Similarly, the EIR projected that the county would need to spend about $1.2 million initially for road construction and improvements in addition to maintenance costs of about $36,000 per year thereafter. It also hinted that one highway would eventually need to be rebuilt and widened at a cost of $3.5 million plus yearly maintenance of $18,000. Yet, by its own figures, Dow estimated that the project, when fully built, would contribute just a little more than $100,000 annually to Solano County's road tax fund.

There were negotiations going on between the county and Dow as to who would bear these costs. There was always the possibility that the county might be able to assess other major industrial land-owners in the area their proportionate share of any money Dow might contribute to road building. But these options were either not mentioned or only vaguely referred to in the EIR.

While Dow officials told me that the complex would attract little additional industrial growth in and of itself, the EIR stated the opposite: "Historically, the existence of a major complex such as proposed has resulted in the generation of new business based partly on support of the new plant and partly as a purchaser of its product for further processing and distribution." Specifically, the EIR said it was "likely that a vinyl chloride polymerization plant would be constructed near the Dow facilities." Other possible downstream facilities identified included polyethylene and polystyrene fabrication and synthetic rubber manufacture. However, the EIR made no attempt to estimate the fiscal impact of these industries nor of that which development of the PG&E, ARCO, Southern Pacific, and National Steel parcels might have.

Given questions regarding the increased cost of county services as well as the impact of associated facilities that might follow Dow, people like Michael Storper would not buy the EIR's confident assertion that: "The Dow facilities, because of their high assessed value per employee, would contribute in property taxes many times the local cost associated with their employees and families."

While these substantive questions worried the opposition, they weren't the whole story. Environmentalists were hopping mad that they had only 30 days to comment on the draft EIR. It was a very practical concern: most opponents of the Dow project were volunteers and they needed more time to gear up for even a superficial review. Larry Silver says Dow's "horrendous, unseemly haste" generated fierce animosity that served to intensify the opposition. Positions were fast hardening, and the opposing sides were talking past one another. A big storm was brewing in the hills.

Chapter 5

THE COUNTY SAYS GO; THE OPPOSITION SAYS NO

Despite the concerns expressed by a handful of environmentalists, there was, in truth, very little hard-core local opposition to Dow's proposed complex. That's not to say people weren't concerned. Sometimes the meeting room was packed, although just as often county officials played to an empty house. Opponents claimed that what might be called the "movers and shakers" syndrome seemed to have affected the populace: as is often the case in smaller communities, when the powers that be are behind a project—there was little doubt that the county board wholeheartedly supported Dow at the time—citizens will usually go along, trusting county officials, their elected representatives, and community leaders to watch out for their interests.

Bill Emmington alleges that the apparent lack of interest was attributable to a lack of notice by the county.

> I believe the planning hearings that related to Dow had about as much publicity as maybe somebody applying for a variance to build a three-car garage. Very few people knew about it; there were no public notices sent down to the people of the Montezuma Hills who would be directly affected by this industry. There were no notices posted, and this is a customary procedure to notify people who are going to be affected by any development.

County officials deny this, noting that no one challenged the legal sufficiency of notice they gave about the project.

By August 1975, things were really rolling and the project seemed to be a sure bet. The draft environmental impact report, begun in February by Solano County, was circulated to the public and local, regional, and state agencies. Dow persuaded the state to speed up its review of the EIR. According to Jack Jones, "The guy at OPR,

Preble Stolz, Bill Press' predecessor, honchoed the EIR through the
state agencies in only 30 days instead of the statutory 45. The state
had a bad reputation in following that law, but we got it through
in record time.''

But, as Larry Silver observes, ''unseemly haste did a great deal
to generate resentment at the early stages.'' Several state agencies
reportedly chafed under this special treatment. Critics also claim
that some agencies had only a week to evaluate the voluminous
study, and that others, influenced by what they perceived as Governor Brown's bias in favor of the project, let the EIR slide through
with little scrutiny. Then, later, when the agencies got a second
chance to comment when the U.S. Army Corps of Engineers prepared an impact statement, they came down hard on the project,
perhaps convinced by then that the Brown Administration was not
pushing the project after all. Another explanation, advanced by
project proponents, is that the state agencies were just lazy, knowing
they would get another chance to review the project in detail when
DOW applied for the necessary state permits.

Aside from raising the hackles of various state agencies, Dow's
haste brought the project to the attention of the state attorney general's crack environmental unit, something the company would sorely
regret. The Attorney General, Evelle Younger, a moderate Republican, had given this unit a free hand to intervene in environmental
disputes without being invited in by another state agency. ''They
were a brilliant bunch of young lawyers,'' says Jack Jones of Dow,
''but a sinister force.'' Jones' view is shared by many others in
California's industrial circles.

Headed first by Nick Yost, later to become chief general counsel
for the Council on Environmental Quality under President Jimmy
Carter, and then by Clem Shute, the environmental unit gained a
well-deserved reputation as hard-nosed advocates for the environment. They were scrappy, tough, and honest, with politics taking
a back seat to environmental protection. They won victory after
stunning victory, expanding the scope of the state's environmental
laws, forcing local governments to pay attention to state land-use
laws, and fighting polluters across California. Larry King, a smart,
energetic deputy attorney general who would be assigned to the
Dow case, described the unit like this: ''We didn't need client
agencies. We were self-generating using the direct authority of the
California Attorney General to come in and file law suits. We were
an activist unit, but above all, we enforced the law.''

Harry Krade, an old hand in the California Department of Agriculture who was upset about the prospect of a Williamson Act contract cancellation, flagged the Dow project for the Attorney General's office. Larry King was brought in to handle the case. King became the proverbial thorn in Dow's side, forcing the company and Solano County to adhere to the letter of the law at every turn. As King recounted:

> The first person I heard from was Harry Krade, a senior, senior staffer in the Department of Agriculture—he helped write the Williamson Act— who was extremely concerned about loss of agricultural land. He was saying, "Hey, isn't this a violation of something. What do you mean they're cancelling a Williamson Act contract?" We didn't get involved in personalities in the Dow case and we didn't have the pleasure of combat. Our job was to make sure things were done right. I prided myself on having an objective view. I was a law and order type. I didn't care whether it was a good or bad project, only that the law was followed. The law would weed out the bad projects.

King says he cringed at reviewing the EIR. "I had been involved at the beginning of CEQA and had seen a lot of big-project EIRs, but none that were so blatantly the developer's EIR. It was a sweetheart EIR that reeked with what was convenient for Dow. You see this in EIRs for little projects, but this was a classic case of the EIR not being written with the proper perspective."

King was disturbed because he thought highly of Jerry Gilbert, who had been hired by Dow to write the EIR.

> Jerry was the former executive officer for the state Water Resources Control Board. He does a very credible job on EIRs. But I heard an awful lot of scuttlebutt that he was under pressure to produce for a big client with big money. But he knew better. Dow's lawyer didn't appear to, though. He . . . knew politicians and the local process, but not the state agencies. Dow's law firm was intransigent in dealing with the state bureaucrats, a little redneck towards them even though many of the people in the agencies were top-notch. Anyway, the thing was just rushed through too fast.

King says that the EIR was written for state review in draft form and contained few exhibits. He also says that Dow asked the time frame to be cut from 45 days to 30.

> At the time I said six months is an appropriate time to review that kind of environmental impact report to make sure the revised one with comments is significantly better. They ran it through in 30 days. Agencies didn't even know what was going on and they were supposed to comment. You know state agencies—they can't even get up to gear in 30

days. The heads of agencies wrote typical bureaucratic letters that said
we reviewed it and that we don't see any serious problems.

Only later, King adds, did state officials like Neil Moyer of the
Air Resources Board raise questions about the emissions from the
proposed Dow facility and their effect on air quality in the Central
Valley. "Those questions were never asked in 30 days," King says.
"Some people didn't even say anything. Only Harry Krade at Agriculture really reviewed it, and it didn't take him long to find all the
problems except the super technical legal ones."

By the end of the 30-day state review, King says, there were
starting to be some noises heard that this was a major project and
that it had some major problems that needed to be looked at. But
state reviews normally cover local projects only if they have regional
significance or if a state agency has to grant permits for it. The
agencies should have made sure the EIR was good, King adds, or
they couldn't use it when it came time to grant the permits.

King, now a real estate investor, says the 30-day review period
was simply unrealistic.

> Why did Dow ask to have the time shortened? Was it funding? Did they
> anticipate problems? There was always a suspicion they were trying to
> hide something. What was the rush? A little real estate developer has
> to go through six months-to-a-year in California. You just factor it into
> your project planning. What's Dow doing in there asking for 30 days?

But what of all the meetings Dow and the county had with state
agency representatives? Why didn't the state people say something?
Why no comments? Because, King asserts, Dow gave them only
30 days and an agency just doesn't respond in that time. "They
have all these EIRs to do and the process is very bureaucratic. The
EIR comes in and it takes two weeks before it even comes out of
the state clearinghouse at OPR heading over to the other agencies
with little computer printouts asking if they're interested in the Dow
project. Most agencies don't even comment, especially if they have
to issue a permit, because they'll have to go over it themselves
later."

I talked with Jerry Gilbert, Dow's consultant, to get his perspective on the EIR flap. As Larry King told me, Gilbert had been
executive director of the California Water Resources Control Board
from 1969 to 1972, and before that he had been head of the San
Francisco Water Quality Board. He left the government in 1972 to
open his own private consulting firm. Gilbert took on some small
projects for Dow, analyzing the environmental impact of several

pipelines, and then was hired to prepare the EIR on the big Collinsville facility.

> We started in the fall of 1974. We had meetings with other concerned
> counties about the potential impact of the facility and the Contra Costa
> staff gave us comments. Considering the size of the project, the schedule
> was tight. We had periods when we were in the office nights and Sundays
> on a continual basis, but we really didn't feel constrained except for
> the first draft of the Corps [of Engineers'] EIR. The level of detail was
> limited somewhat by time, but you know how work expands if the time
> is there.

However, several people who reviewed drafts of the EIR say that
when they pointed out problems to Gilbert, he and his employees
countered with stories about the terrible time pressures they were
under.

Even more serious a charge was that Gilbert's work was not
independent of Dow's control. His voice rises slightly when responding to such charges. "I always felt I was reporting to the
county and, more importantly, to my own conscience. Dow did
push on the timing, but that was their only influence. At the time,
the EIR was state of the art, what I felt was necessary, and what
the client—Solano County—needed. We did a fine job. Anyway,
the new arrangement [where prospective EIR consultants have their
names placed on a county list] doesn't eliminate bias. The consultants all know what a particular county wants and write their
EIRs accordingly."

Like others, Gilbert is critical of the state agencies for responding
so slowly.

> The state agencies simply didn't have their act together. They didn't set
> up review schedules so that their actions were consistent. If the state
> felt this was really a major decision, then OPR should have gotten
> involved, but there was no direction from the state, especially from the
> perspective of saying this is a project to keep an eye on. Some state
> agencies, particularly agriculture and the Air Resources Board, saw in
> the EIR process an opportunity to get more than information. They
> converted it from an information-gathering process to a decision-making
> process and demanded information of such scientific depth that it would
> have required original research. They raised a lot of questions about the
> EIR, and we assured them they would be answered in the Corps' EIS.
> Solano County believed this so they approved the EIR. But when the
> federal process began, the state torpedoed it.

Thus, even though the state agencies had signed off for now, it was clear that Dow was headed for trouble. "But Dow could have corrected everything except maybe the Williamson Act problems," says Larry King. "They could have changed the comprehensive plan and rewritten the EIR. We flagged every issue. Clem Shute and I even sat down with Solano County and explained exactly what sort of findings were required to cancel the Williamson Act contract. They didn't even know they had to make certain findings, but the county ended up blowing it anyway."

Dow and Solano County were undaunted for now; the project seemed to have momentum. After the state agencies had signed off on the EIR, Contra Costa County concurred and by December 1975, the Solano County Board of Supervisors had certified that the EIR was an adequate assessment of all environmental impacts and that the project would have no significant adverse environmental effects.

Richard Brann and Dow both say the final draft of the EIR addressed the concerns of the environmentalists from San Francisco, Berkeley, and Sacramento in great detail. Dow felt confident. It exercised the short-term option that it held on the McOmie Ranch. Ray Brubaker would later look back and observe, "We were naive to assume that because we had gotten across the first hurdle of the EIR we were safe. We bought the land too quickly. A longer-term option would have been wiser."

Solano County was confident too. Having certified the EIR, the county board wasted no time rezoning 834 acres of the Collinsville site from agricultural to industrial use. It also cancelled that part of the Williamson Act contract applicable to the rezoned property, which made it necessary under state law to demonstrate that alternative sites (those that didn't require the conversion of agricultural or open space) were not available, and that the change in use from agriculture to industrial would benefit agriculture. Dow paid $230,000 in Williamson Act contract cancellation fees to the state of California and negotiated an agreement with Solano County to maintain roads to the site during construction. Somewhat belatedly, Solano County started drawing up a specific industrial development plan for the Collinsville area, focusing primarily on transportation needs and utility services.

To everyone's surprise, the project was moving along nicely, even a bit ahead of schedule. Now that Dow had triple-jumped adroitly over the local requirements, it was set to apply for necessary air quality permits from the Bay Area Air Pollution Control District (BAAPCD) and approvals from state agencies and the U.S. Army Corps of Engineers.

But environmentalists didn't like the way the final EIR sounded nor the way it had been handled, particularly the fact that Dow contracted directly with the consultant who was supposed to make an unbiased analysis of the project. They felt the rezoning was flatly contrary to established California law because the county did not contemplate this type of industrial development on the McOmie land. Further, some thought that the Williamson Act contract had been cancelled improperly.

Fearing that the county's actions would establish damaging precedents on these three points, Friends of the Earth, the Sierra Club, and a San Francisco group called People for Open Space filed suit on December 19, 1975, just beating the deadline for challenging the county's actions. Dow, joined by a covey of politicians and labor leaders, reacted violently to the lawsuit, painting it as another obstructionist strategy by no-growthers from San Francisco. But Larry Silver, the Sierra Club attorney who was in charge of the case, vigorously defends the suit on its merits.

Silver, a bushy-haired, middle-aged man who wears the continually harried, somewhat dishevelled look of a busy litigator, works out of a noisy office overlooking California Street in San Francisco. Tall stacks of paper cover his desk, some leaning at odd angles, almost as if tempting an earthquake. The phone rings constantly.

At first, Silver didn't remember much about the Dow case. He says he doesn't have the luxury of looking back or following developments once a case is closed. But it didn't take him long to warm to the subject when he heard that Dow people had said this was just another obstructionist suit.

> The case wasn't frivolous. We had excellent legal issues—none of the issues were specious. We had a good argument on the EIR, but that wasn't necessarily the main focus. Don't forget that two of the three points in the suit—the rezoning and Williamson Act cancellation—had nothing to do with environmental impact assessment. They were issues we could have gotten reviewed a number of years ago, and there is nothing unique in California about seeking judicial review of administrative agency action in a land-use context. It's been going on for years. I didn't see it as an example of environmentalists being able to slow down the process. That's the kind of thing that industrial and residential sites have been subject to for some time. After all, we do have a system whereby the courts can review an administrative permit.

Larry King agrees with Silver's assessment.

> In my mind it was the perfect model of a good environmental law suit.

My office even got to the point of quoting odds. We thought it was a 90 percent winner on the EIR issues. It was about a 75-80 percent winner on the general plan issue. The plan was an amateur one, a good example of small county planning. It had glaring inconsistencies—divergent policy issues on the same point. It was clear there was no industrial development contemplated on the site for at least 10 years. The Williamson Act was the hardest one but probably the most significant. The county blew it on the findings question. We told Dow and the county in a courtesy letter "Do make findings. We'd hate to see you lose it if you didn't make findings. The law is clear in California that you have to." The county had 13 pages of findings, but left out one-half the findings required, so they probably would have lost on that, too, and wouldn't have gotten to the merits of the Williamson Act issue about alternative sites.

But Dow and the county believed they had justified the cancellation, conjuring up benefits that lesser imaginations might have overlooked. Dow argued that the new plants would benefit agriculture by producing the raw material for plastic parts to be used on tractors and other farm machinery. Dow also pointed out that some of the chemicals would end up in fertilizers.

To top things off, farmer McOmie was persuaded to put $5 million from the sale of his land into a trust fund for agricultural purchases. Art Shelton had this to say: "The purchase price on the property— $5 million of the $6 million purchase price as a matter of fact— went into a trust. It went to University of California-Davis and Cal Poly [California Polytechnic State University] for agricultural research. I defy anybody to point to any place in the world where you get from land like that as much benefit for agriculture as actually resulted from taking this thing out of the Williamson Act. That's going to benefit agriculture all over this state in huge quantities."

Larry King shakes his head at these arguments.

> There was quirky language in the law that said you could cancel if there were no other suitable alternative sites. The question was what was the sphere of that suitable alternative site—the fact that there was no other site right next door to their plant or that there were no alternative sites in northern California? We took the position, informally, that doesn't mean that something doesn't happen to be available next door to you. It's more than just your convenience as a developer. Then there was the issue of what was a compatible use. Building a tomato processing plant adjacent to a tomato field, that's one thing. Is that a compatible use? That issue is unresolved under our law. Dow was trying to argue that they made fertilizers and that was a compatible use.

King chuckles at the last thought.

But if the case was as strong as King seems to think, why didn't the attorney general bring suit? Dow gave me a letter sent by Younger to Richard Brann in March 1976 that said while the attorney general believed the county's action raised "substantial legal questions," he did "not think the county's position on these issues is sufficiently lacking in merit to compel us to take action on our own initiative."

King smiles. Despite the usual hands-off policy Younger had towards the environmental unit, apparently politics did play a part. He says that Younger, a Republican who aspired to be governor, told the environmental unit he would sue Solano County and Dow on behalf of Governor Brown, a Democrat, and one of his agencies, but not on his own. "Why should I take the flack?" Younger reportedly asked. In any case, King says he had red-flagged every issue for all to see. Richard Brann adds that King made the county sign a waiver that would allow the Attorney General to sue later if he wanted to.

Jack Jones claims King did more than just red-flag issues. "Younger's attorneys were perceived by us to be working surreptitiously with the Sierra Club, doing legal research for them. We gave serious consideration to trying to get a grand jury to look at this, but were persuaded not to because Younger was going to run for governor." Both King and Silver vehemently deny these allegations. King retorts that he scrupulously maintained a distance from the Sierra Club and other environmental groups. "Some others in the office had memberships in these groups. I didn't belong to any of them. Our office uncovered all the problems, but we gave nothing to Larry Silver." But even Bill Press, Governor Brown's former planning advisor, says there was a link between Silver and King. "Larry was, behind the scenes, involved in the Sierra Club lawsuit. I don't want to accuse him of that but I think it is true that he was, at least informally."

There is no doubt, however, that environmentalists got help from state agencies throughout the fight against Dow. "We had a running joke about almost having an underground government," Cynthia Kay told me, "because so many of our people were on state phone lines or knew state people. It really helped on the phone bills and getting ahold of state people."

In fact, there are many conservation-minded people working in state government in California. I have seen the system work myself when I was involved in an environmental lawsuit in the state. I was on the side of the "good guys" and, consequently, state employees went far beyond the call of duty to cooperate, giving me information that I might have had to file suit to get out of bureaucrats in more development-oriented jurisdictions. Nothing illegal, mind you, just very cooperative.

But whether Larry Silver did it on his own or with help from King, he wasted no time in filing suit and causing Dow trouble. "We had reason to believe that there was information about environmental damage that came to Gilbert's attention that didn't get into the EIR at Dow's request. There were rumors, some emanating from Gilbert and Associates—we had some conversations with some of their people who left—that all was not kosher in the EIR process."

Silver tried to get that information from Dow by filing a motion to talk with Jerry Gilbert and to get certain internal documents. But Dow, which had brought in new attorneys from Los Angeles to represent it, refused to turn any information over. "They chose a litigation strategy that could only result in delay," claims Silver.

> Dow might counter that to allow discovery would have caused delay, but not the year's delay we ultimately got. The law suit was all tied up in knots on this issue. That was their doing, not ours. And I suppose one can always ask the improper lawyer's point that if they didn't have anything to hide, why didn't they just let us take Gilbert's deposition? True, we did appeal all the way to the California Supreme Court on the discovery issue, but the court ultimately vindicated our position. This took such a long time that by the time we got the discovery issue decided, the project was dead.

Chapter 6

BAAPCD LETS THE AIR OUT OF DOW

Dow didn't let the Sierra Club suit slow it down a bit. With local approvals in hand, the company moved confidently to get permits from regional, state, and federal agencies. Most crucial were air pollution permits from the Bay Area Air Pollution Control District (BAAPCD, now known as the Bay Area Air Quality Management District, or BAAQMD) for the styrene plant, which Dow would build first. Jack Jones claims the project team met with BAAPCD staff early in 1974 and got assurances that Dow would have no problems. "They told us that San Francisco was not classified as a non-attainment area and that there would be no such designation in the foreseeable future."

This was a crucial point because if an area didn't have air that was clean enough to meet federal ambient air standards for pollutants, such as particulates and hydrocarbons, then it didn't make any difference how few emissions a plant had. The law of the land—the Clean Air Act—at that time forbade issuance of a permit to construct a new facility in areas with dirty air.

Milton Feldstein, then second in command at BAAPCD and now chief, says he's amazed at Jones' assertion. "The area's air pollution problems were well-known at the time. We've had a comprehensive air monitoring system in the Bay Area since 1957. Thirty stations for ozone, 18 for particulates, and 15 for nitrous oxide. There was no place in the Bay Area, except maybe San Francisco, that didn't exceed federal standards."

Public records support Feldstein on this point. BAAPCD was forced to adopt regulations for new facilities in 1972 because the region did not meet national standards for several pollutants. But perhaps Dow did have reason to believe something could be worked out. Everyone involved, including environmentalists, recognized that Dow would use advanced technology to control air pollution and that the plant would be squeaky clean when compared with older styrene facilities in other states. Jack Jones is a bit more graphic in his assessment. "The sheep grazing on the property would have farted more petrochemicals in the air than this plant would have emitted."

Not only was the plant clean, but BAAPCD and its then-head, D.J. (Jud) Callaghan, had a reputation for being "flexible." In 15 years on the job, one writer says, Callaghan had denied only 36 permits and that most of those denials came in the 1970s when state and federal officials put pressure on him for more vigorous enforcement.[17] In fairness to Callaghan, BAAPCD did not have a permit system until 1976; on the other hand, the same month that Dow filed for its permits Callaghan was defending himself against charges by Nathaniel Flynn, a senior BAAPCD staff engineer, who alleged the district management had shown favoritism toward big industrial polluters. The district's directors, in a 12-5 vote, held that Flynn's complaints were "without merit."

The Bay Area Air Pollution Control District was established in 1955, the first regional agency of its type in California. Encompassing nine counties, including the part of Solano where the Dow site was to be located, BAAPCD was given the job of enforcing national and state air quality laws applicable to all sources of air pollution, except cars and trucks. That power rested with the California Air Resources Board (ARB).

The district is governed by an 18-member board of directors with representatives chosen from elected members of county boards and city councils throughout the region on a per capita basis. Callaghan, Feldstein and about 200 others work for the board, running BAAPCD on a day-to-day basis, reviewing applications, issuing and denying permits, and enforcing regulations and standards established by the board. These standards generally follow state and federal requirements. Anyone not happy with the district's decisions or who has been cited for violating a standard can appeal to an independent five-member hearing board.

BAAPCD was praised by Paul DeFalco, the respected former head of EPA's regional office in San Francisco, as "the most responsible district in the state." It was one of few local air agencies that had been allowed to write its own rules for review of new sources of pollution. Most other regions in California had their rules written for them either by the ARB or EPA. BAAPCD's rules included a provision that directed denial of any new application like Dow's if the project "emitted a significant quantity of any air contaminant that would interfere with attainment or maintenance of any air quality standard.''

Even though BAAPCD had been around for a long time, in some ways the agency was playing a new game. It was having trouble reconciling pressures for more growth with the Bay Area's already dirty air and tough new state and national air pollution laws. The heat was on Callaghan not only to clean up the region's air, but also to approve projects that would provide jobs.

The way the law was written, however, there was very little room to maneuver. One key idea behind the national Clean Air Act was to clean up areas that failed to meet minimum national standards set to protect human health. To accomplish this goal, the act embraced a concept never tried anywhere else in the world—ambient air standards—in addition to emission limits.

Dow was to be the guinea pig. ''Dow had two tests to satisfy,'' Milt Feldstein explains. ''First, did it meet applicable emission limits? If those limits were met, then the second inquiry was whether it put out enough pollution to make the region's air noticeably worse and thereby interfere with eventual attainment of national ambient air standards we had to follow.'' If it did, Feldstein says, BAAPCD had no choice but to deny the permit. Dow passed the first step with flying colors, but Feldstein claims the company didn't seem to understand what ambient air standards were all about. ''They thought that having the 'cleanest plant possible' would be good enough. It was a strategic error.''

Thus, BAAPCD was caught up in a seemingly impossible task: How could it clean up the air as required by federal law if it allowed new polluters into the Bay Area? Unfortunately, Congress had provided virtually no guidance on how it might pull off such a magical feat.

On May 4, 1976, Dow formally submitted its request to BAAPCD for permits to build the styrene plant. Dow asked that the styrene plant, one of the least polluting petrochemical processes, be considered as a free-standing unit rather than as a part of a larger complex. The styrene plant would emit four major pollutants: particulates—small pieces of ash and dust that result from combustion and can cause lung damage; sulfur dioxide—also a by-product of combustion that has been linked with respiratory problems in humans; and nitrous oxide and organic emissions that mix with air and sunlight to form smog, the bane of California.

Dow was told it would need a total of 26 air pollution permits for the styrene facility—13 construction and 13 operating permits for each emission point, boilers, superheaters, vacuum vents, and the like in the plant. Two other emission points would have put out little, if any, air contaminants and thus did not fall under the district's regulations.

But fate, once more in the form of ARCO, struck again. Even though the company had not completed an environmental impact analysis, ARCO had earlier applied for air pollution permits for the $1 billion petrochemical complex it wanted to build upstream from Dow—the same project that had precipitated environmentalists' fears of a Ruhr Valley effect along the Sacramento. The day before Dow submitted its application BAAPCD flatly denied ARCO a permit because, in Feldstein's words, "its emissions would have been way out of line. They would have exceeded ambient air standards by a huge margin and emission limits by up to 146 times for sulfur dioxide."

ARCO slunk away quietly saying it would have to reevaluate whether the project could be built under such severe restrictions. This was the twelfth application BAAPCD had turned down on ambient air grounds. Little political hay was made of this denial even though the ARCO complex would have employed more people and produced more tax revenue than the new Dow facility. But the damage was done. As next in line, Dow became a focal point for environmentalists who saw a looming threat to the region's air quality, for unions that perceived a growing threat to jobs, and to businessmen who got the message that industry wasn't especially welcome in California.

In this atmosphere, BAAPCD began processing Dow's application. Its engineering division, finding that each of the emission points would meet district standards, gave the plant its imprimatur. However, the engineering division cautioned that some of the emissions did exceed their respective "significance thresholds" as set by district regulations, so that they might affect air quality standards. It recommended that the research and planning division review the application from this perspective.

The research and planning division did so, and balked at approving the project. The research and planning people had developed a computer model that showed the styrene plant would contribute significant and measurable ground-level increments of particulates, mainly non-methane hydrocarbons and oxidants. Emissions of sulfur dioxide and nitrogen dioxide were also found to be significant, but not to the point where air quality standards for these two pollutants would have been exceeded.

Because the Montezuma Hills area already violated the state and federal air quality standards for particulates, hydrocarbons, and oxidants, the planning division felt compelled to deny the application in accord with the district's Regulation 2, Division 1309, which prohibited authorization of any new facility "which may cause the emission or creation of a significant quantity of any air contaminant which would interfere with the attainment or maintenance of any air quality standard." In making a preliminary recommendation of denial, the planning division made it clear that in its opinion this wasn't even a close case. "Particulate and organic emissions are well over the detection thresholds, by factors of 4.7 and 5.3 respectively."

July 8, 1976, was a big day for Jud Callaghan. Dow wasn't the only thing on his mind. Alameda County Supervisor Tom Bates was spearheading a drive to reform the district's operations—and he wanted to get Callaghan out. Bates contended that the board had abdicated its responsibilities in summarily dismissing Nathaniel Flynn's charges against Callaghan. Bates argued that Callaghan's removal was a necessary first step toward a reorganization of the district. James Lemos, a Benicia city councilman, pointing out that formal complaints accusing Callaghan of mismanagement went back to 1972, defended his chief. "In every case the board has dismissed the charges. The air in the Bay Area is getting cleaner and the district should be defending that. The polluters' best friends are those who are harassing the district." A majority of the district board agreed with Lemos and voted 11-4 to retain Callaghan. On another vote, however, the board agreed to have the agency's staff analyze Bates' proposals for revising district operations and tightening enforcement practices.

Some critics say that Bates' attack put Callaghan on the run and that Dow was simply in the wrong place at the wrong time. BAAPCD officials deny this, pointing out that the numbers for particulate and organic emissions clearly violated the district's regulations. So, on July 8, Jud Callaghan issued a preliminary denial of the styrene plant applications. Jack Jones says confident Dow executives were stunned. They met with Callaghan and Feldstein on July 19 where, as Jones says:

> We found out for the first time and to our great surprise that they had calculated that the air at that site exceeded federal ambient air standards one day out of the year. And under federal rules you can't give a permit for any new source that has a "significant" amount of emissions. They [the federal government] didn't define the word "significant" so the district board said since we have no instructions from Congress or the

EPA as to what significant is, we will say it's one molecule. We said
fine, we can meet that standard because at that particular time it was
what you could measure at the plant boundary line. We knew you would
not be able to detect the emissions of that plant at the boundary line.
You could calculate it, but not measure it. So they [BAAPCD] said,
"Oh no, we're going to change that rule too. That no longer applies.
What you've got to do is figure it at the stack and inside the plant."
We said OSHA [Occupational Safety and Health Administration] regs
apply there, but they denied our permit on that basis.

Milt Feldstein, who has been at BAAPCD for 22 years, comes
across as the quintessential administrator/regulator—not too flashy
and definitely not someone you'd likely ask out for a beer on Friday
after work. But you know intuitively he would doggedly enforce
the rules as he reads them. "I take the law seriously. Many people
don't. We don't care where a plant goes as long as it meets the
standards. You could put a coal-fired plant in downtown San Francisco if it can meet the standards."

Feldstein agrees with part of what Jones says. But some emotion
creeps into his voice when he hears that Dow claims BAAPCD
changed the rules in midstream.

I can't believe that kind of statement because I know I participated in
at least a dozen meetings with Dow, even before they submitted an
application. We tried to explain what the ground rules were. We went
over it quite thoroughly with them. If you could measure the emissions
on a monitor at ground level, then it was significant. For example, with
particulates you can measure 5 micrograms per cubic meter so anything
above that was "significant." That was our innovative approach, now
in use elsewhere, in determining what "significant" meant. That was
a regulation adopted by our board of directors in 1972, not a state law.
It was adopted under the Clean Air Act Amendments of 1970. We had
one of the first new source review rules to be adopted by a local agency
and approved by EPA. We had no choice but to deny the application.

Dow and its supporters say Callaghan's and Feldstein's discomfort
was self-created. They point out that while the district board had
indeed adopted the regulation that forbids construction of any facility
with significant emissions that might interfere with attainment of
air quality standards, it was left up to Callaghan to define what
"significant" was and that he went off the deep end. Even Bill
Press, who had taken over the governor's Office of Planning and
Research, is critical. "The regional boards are autonomous and can
adopt stronger regulations than the state requires. The state can't
step in and say this is unreasonable or demand uniformity. The

district was going overboard.''

Jack Jones rails that the measurement technique the district adopted almost guaranteed that emissions from any plant would be ''significant.'' ''They kept piling up the worst possible conditions into the same time period and justified it on the basis that the standard must not be exceeded even one day a year under the worst possible conditions.'' There is some truth to this. Predicting the effect of emissions from a new plant is a very tricky business. The process is called modeling and is done with the help of computers. In a nutshell, analysts take the projected emissions from a plant, plug in assumptions about things such as wind speed and the terrain of the area, and, voila, out comes a prediction of how those emissions will affect air quality at various points in the region. The process is becoming more sophisticated with experience, but it is far from scientific.

The district used computer modeling to determine if Dow's emissions would be ''significant.'' It first calculated what the maximum ground level concentration of a pollutant would be from each of the plant's emission points and then added them. If this gave a pollution level that could theoretically be detected by an air quality monitor, then the district ruled the amount was significant and denied the permit. But, as Dow experts pointed out, it was a scientific impossibility that there would be one point on the ground where one would find a maximum amount of pollution from every smoke stack in the plant, even though that is precisely what the district assumed when it simply added the maximum values. District officials concede that this approach overstated the amount of pollution, but dismissed criticism saying it was a ''safety factor penalty.''

Dow people were particularly irked because many jurisdictions across the state and country had adopted, with EPA approval, numerical definitions of ''significant'' pollution by establishing a review cut-off value for each important pollutant. If an anticipated emission from a new source fell below the cut-off number, often set at 150 lbs/hour, the impact of the emission was deemed ''insignificant.'' Dow thought it could satisfy such a numerical limit.

Jones and others also point out, accurately, that in other areas of the country that were supposed to be operating under the same laws new plants were being built and that the California Air Resources Board had developed a model trade-off regulation with EPA's blessing, but that BAAPCD refused to amend their regulations. ''We tried to get them to consider the two plants as one integrated facility separated by a river because we didn't have room on the Pittsburg side,'' Jones explains. ''The two are going to be connected with pipe lines, so if you judge the two as one facility we could trade off by reducing emissions at the existing plant in Pittsburg. We said, 'Hey look, if you'll let us reduce emissions at the Pittsburg site we can trade-off that against any new emissions from the styrene plant.'''

But Feldstein claims that he and Callaghan had very little flexibility to deal with Dow. ''You must remember that we didn't have the kind of trade-off or offset provision Dow wanted in our district regulations. We did recognize trade-offs between the same company and on the same site, but not the liberalized kind Dow talked about— its sites were four miles apart. The regulations simply said that if emissions interfered with the attainment or maintenance of air quality standards then we had to deny the project.''

Feldstein argues that if BAAPCD would have allowed Dow to clean up its Pittsburg facility in exchange for the right to add emissions to the air from the styrene plant, it would have been in violation of local and perhaps federal law and open to legal action. ''EPA was working on an interpretive ruling to allow such offsets, but it wasn't clear if such a procedure was legal. Later, in December 1977, the California Air Resources Board did adopt a new source review rule allowing offsets as now allowed under the Clean Air Act Amendments.''

Ironically, when the district did allow Standard Oil to undertake even a limited intra-company trade-off on a low-sulfur and fuel oil unit, Feldstein says that BAAPCD took a lot of abuse. Seems like regulators can't win. Bill Press says the state was also frustrated by this attitude. ''BAAPCD was a regional agency we could do nothing about. They were independent. The governor couldn't do anything. He couldn't fire anyone.''

Whether or not BAAPCD had leeway on the offsets questions, Feldstein says the issue of whether emissions should have been measured at the plant boundary or at the point of emission is a red herring. ''We and our board have taken the view that, as far as ambient air quality standards are concerned, they apply anywhere— on the property or off. The maximum particulate matter concentration was highest on their property, but in terms of organics and nitrogen oxides the highest was off their property, so that issue was really irrelevant.''

But a close look at the case shows that Dow may have indeed found a loophole, at least with respect to particulate matter from the plant. BAAPCD and EPA regulations stated that for purposes of determining whether ambient air standards would be violated, calculations would be outside the property boundary of the plant, where the public had access. Dow purchased a huge amount of excess land, ostensibly for a greenbelt area around the plant to insulate neighbors from any problems and also for possible future expansion. But it was now clear Dow had a third very good reason for the buffer zone—to side-step air pollution problems, albeit legally, by simply excluding the public from a large area around its facility. Environmentalists don't like to admit that Dow outfoxed them on this point, but it was not until 1980 that EPA moved to close this loophole, which other polluters around the country have also attempted to exploit.

On the other hand, Feldstein correctly points out that the property line squabble was irrelevant with regard to other pollutants, particularly ones like hydrocarbons that react with other substances to form smog. The real effect, as one district official explained, may not be at the plant at all. Indeed, it may be outside their property. The real effect is downwind somewhere after the chemical reactions have taken place. On this ground alone, some attorneys say, Callaghan was justified in rejecting Dow's application.

Given these diametrically opposed positions, it is no wonder little progress was made at the July 14 meeting. That set the stage for a boisterous public hearing on the denial held by BAAPCD on July 19 at the Solano County seat in Fairfield. The very fact of a public hearing on a specific industrial project near its site was a break with past district practices. It was Tom Bates' idea, endorsed by environmental groups, the California Air Resources Board, and Callaghan as a means to ensure full and open discussion of the Dow plant.

Big Jud Callaghan, crewcut and looking as solid and immovable as the college football player and U.S. Marine he once was, presided over the hearing. He gazed out over an audience that included 600 construction workers and others wearing hard hats and carrying signs reading "JOBS NEEDED, NOT UNEMPLOYMENT; OPEN YOUR EYES; JOBS, NOT WELFARE; POLITICIANS HAVE GUARANTEED SALARIES." Environmentalists were lost in the crowd, vastly outnumbered by the raucous construction workers. Ray Brubaker got a heavy round of applause when he asked Callaghan to reconsider the permit. "We sincerely believe no other styrene plant in the world—operating or proposed—has lower emissions than the one we presented." Brubaker went on to criticize the air district staff for relying on "intuitive reasoning" in analyzing the Dow project. Solano County representatives also weighed in, in favor of the project.

When Milt Feldstein presented the district's side of the story, he was booed. Callaghan tried to explain to Dow's vocal supporters that his decision had to be based on air quality considerations alone. Economic factors like jobs and tax revenues didn't fit into the equation. The hardhats booed and stomped and hooted their disapproval some more. There was a barrage of jeers when Colleen Greenlaw, director of public health for Sacramento County, submitted a resolution from the county Board of Supervisors, which called for rejection of the project unless all air quality requirements were met. Sacramento feared that pollution from Dow would be blown up north, where the city already had serious air pollution problems.

Dow continued to negotiate with BAAPCD. On July 21, the district directors met to hear from Angelo Siracusa, head of the Bay Area Council, a major business organization that is a moderate force in Bay Area politics. Siracusa told those assembled that Callaghan probably made the right decision in view of federal and state laws he had to apply. "But you ought to consider whether you shouldn't have more flexibility in terms of those rules," Siracusa added, arguing that "economic and political factors deserved equal weight with air quality. The air district in effect has become the land-use agency for the Bay Area and probably put the lid on economic development." Still Callaghan held firm. Health considerations were paramount and if people didn't like the law then get Congress to amend it.

In early August, Dow representatives asked Callaghan and Feldstein to take another look at the case. They said the District had made mistakes in calculating organic emissions from the plant. But BAAPCD held firm, rejecting the company's data because it did not take into account organic emissions from ships transferring raw materials and chemicals at Dow's new plant. On August 12, BAAPCD reaffirmed its earlier denial of the styrene plant application, saying it had no choice under existing laws. That left Dow with two options. It could appeal Callaghan's decision to the district's hearing board or submit a new application that would cut particulate and organic emissions below the "detectable" threshold by adding more pollution control equipment.

But even though Dow appeared to be in serious trouble, there was little jubilation among environmentalists. Some, such as Nick Arguimbau, thought the whole air permit process had been a set-up by Callaghan to make the air laws look bad. "Callaghan marshalled his own opposition. He told everyone this was cleaner than a freeway interchange and yet he had to refuse the application. Some people in the agency were going around saying that they didn't think anything could be built under their rules." Anne Jackson, a freelance writer out of Sacramento who followed the Dow case, also questioned Callaghan's motives. "Callaghan chose to deny Dow's permit on the basis of the plant's expected emissions, even though worse polluters are being allowed to operate. The result makes Dow look persecuted and the district arbitrary—perhaps strengthening the company's basis for appeal."[18]

These claims are difficult to prove and almost impossible to refute. The fact of the matter was that Callaghan and Feldstein rendered their decision without delay, none of the waffling industry critics so often accuse regulators of, and they enforced the letter of the law. Whether that law made any sense in practice was a question that would have to be answered—and answered soon.

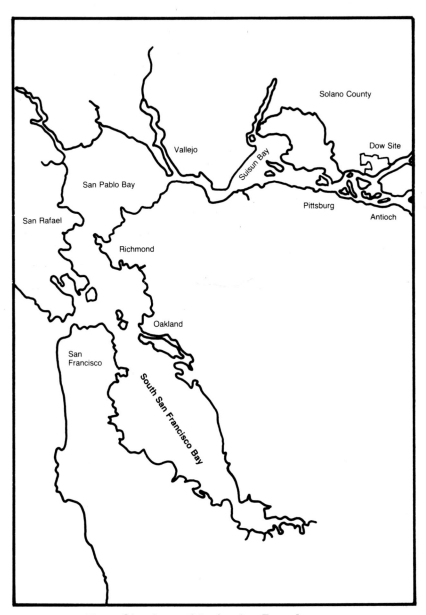

Dow Site Location in the Bay Area

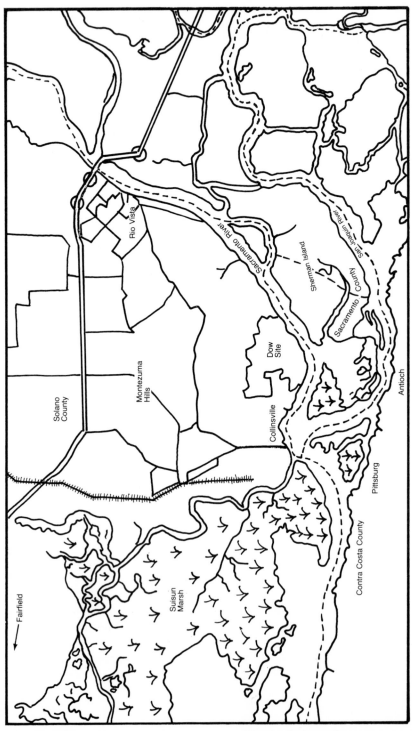

Location of Collinsville and Dow Site in Solano County

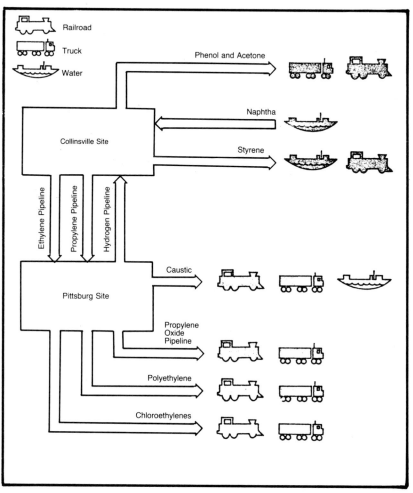

Dow Facility Products and Raw Materials

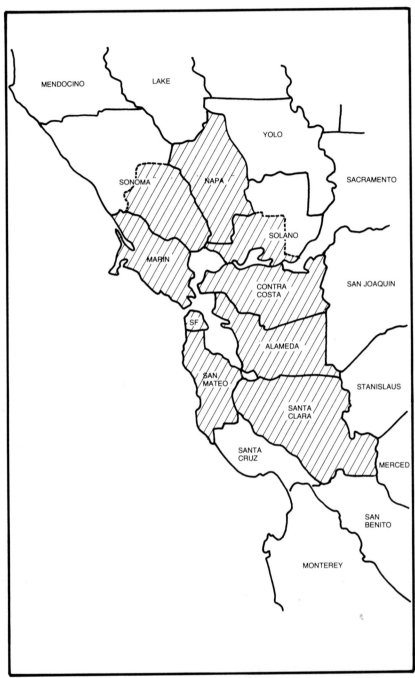

Jurisdiction of Bay Area Air Pollution Control District

Collinsville waterfront at the turn of the century.

Artist's conception of proposed Dow petrochemical facility (photo provided by Dow).

Farmland in the Montezuma Hills near Dow site.

Collinsville graveyard with industrial development in background.

Suisun Marsh.

Oaks and power line atop Montezuma Hills above the Dow site.

Chapter 7

DOW AGONISTES

Dow pulled back to lick its wounds but as one official said: "We haven't given up; we're looking at the alternatives." Things were, however, starting to sour. Earlier in the year, soon after its EIR got the O.K. from Solano County, Dow filed for the state and federal permits and approvals required before it could start construction. Many of these permits had little to do with environmental protection: a dam safety permit from the California Department of Water Resources for the holding pond it would build, permission from the California Reclamation Board to alter existing levees along the Sacramento, and an easement from the California Lands Commission to build a dock and water intake on and to run pipelines over state lands. Dow had to get similar approvals from the U.S. Army Corps of Engineers for construction of the dock and ship-turning basin, the water supply intake, four pipelines, and the wastewater discharge pipe, plus an easement to build these facilities on Corps-owned land that had been used as a dump for dredge spoils.

The crucial environmental permits involved water. Dow needed a half dozen permits from the Regional Water Board to discharge effluents from the plant and to construct the evaporation ponds and sanitary treatment facilities. Even more critical was approval from the State Water Resources Control Board to withdraw scarce water from the Sacramento River (the project would require a lot of water, enough to supply a city of 40,000 people). The California Fish and Game Department also had a say because Dow needed permits from it to alter the riverbed for the dock, water intake and pipelines, all of which could affect nearby wildlife sanctuaries.

Dow also needed a federal water quality permit. Since California had not yet been delegated authority to administer federal water pollution control laws (the state applied its own law at the time), Dow had to get a water pollution discharge permit from the Corps of Engineers. That and the other federal permits triggered NEPA, which required the Corps to file an environmental impact statement (EIS). Because the federal law did not make provision for substituting the already-prepared state EIR for the federal document, the Corps had to prepare a separate document.

As it had done with Solano County, Dow started out like a thoroughbred. Within a few weeks it received the permits it needed from the California Fish and Game Department. Things went quickly, too, with the Corps of Engineers. By April 1975, the Corps had prepared its EIS and scheduled a public hearing for June. But this was the high water mark for Dow, the last substantial forward movement it would make on the project.

People in several state agencies came to the conclusion that they had been hoodwinked when the Dow project was rushed through the EIR review process. Two who were asking the toughest questions, Neil Moyer of the Air Resources Board and Harry Krade of Agriculture, were from agencies that didn't have any permitting power in the case. But their qualms made the others uneasy. Could they ask another round of questions even though the state EIR was approved? Should an agency like the Reclamation Board consider all the environmental consequences of the project, such as impacts on air and land use, even if they didn't fall within an agency's statutory purview?

The Corps' EIS was a perfect opportunity to jump back in. If the state EIR couldn't be reopened, then the federal EIS process was the place to get a second bite. And what a second bite. On March 1, 1976, Gary Weatherford, the deputy secretary of the California Resources Agency (a super department that includes all of the state agencies Dow needed permits from) wrote a six-page letter to the Corps' district engineer detailing myriad of problems the state saw with the project. Weatherford focused on four impacts of critical concern: air quality, increased ship traffic, secondary growth, and chemical spills and water quality. He asked that the Corps "not grant a permit until the State is satisfied that the potential environmental problems can and will be adequately resolved."

Jack Jones shakes his head as he recounts the slide downhill.

Jerry Brown decided to run for President. He lost a lot of interest in what was happening here. Bill Press, Tom Quinn, and most of his key people that could make things happen were preoccupied by the candidacy. So the burden fell to the California Resources Agency, which was headed by Claire Dedrick. She had been a vice-president of the Sierra Club and brought Sierra Club politics with her into public office. The California Resources Agency is the advocacy group for the organized environmental boys. The Corps of Engineers had started its procedures and, to the amazement of us all, Claire Dedrick sent her chief deputy down asking the Corps not to act because the state had a lot of unanswered questions over which the state really had no jurisdiction to look into. The Corps said to us, "Gee, we could go ahead as a matter of law, but as a matter of policy we don't want to proceed if the state takes a position as strong as it's done." We knew we we were in trouble. The questions were quite impossible. Totally philosophical questions. You couldn't answer then with facts.

According to Jones, Dow tried to reach Governor Brown, but to no avail. As Jones puts it:

Our attempts to get his attention were unsuccessful. The governor felt he had dealt with this issue and helped it when we got the EIR through quickly. The negotiations with Dedrick's people were very frustrating. One of the agencies we had to get permits from was the Reclamation Board. Their jurisdiction was limited solely toward being sure that our pipeline crossing the levee was up to code—purely a ministerial function. However, through the encouragement of Claire Dedrick and Larry King— these were private phone calls and that sort of thing—the Reclamation Board was told that, "Hey, even though the EIR has been certified you nevertheless are required by CEQA to consider all of the environmental consequences of your decision. Therefore, you need to inquire what is the impact of this project on the air, water, on the schools"—you name it. They really didn't know how to proceed with that kind of advice.

Jones claims that Dow tried to soothe Dedrick and her people, but to no avail. "We met many, many times with Dedrick's staff and the Air Resources Board staff, and they kept saying we need more information. For example, they wanted to know what the impact of our project will be in the communities of our customers in 1985. Who will your customers be? How will you ship it? What will be their alternatives in the area?" Jones chuckles with a tinge of pain, "These were impossible questions. We didn't even know who our customers would be in 1985 or what volumes they would buy. We answered what questions we could. I was spending at that time $200,000 per month on outside consultants to answer questions and do studies."

State agency officials give a slightly different version. Neil Moyer says it was "like pulling teeth to get information out of Dow. They say they don't have enough design details completed to give a breakdown of hydrocarbon emissions. But if that's so, how can they give us any emission figures at all?" Dr. Robert Pratt, a scientist with the Department of Food and Agriculture, says he had trouble finding out whether the plant would regularly emit ethylene, a plant-aging hormone. "I raised the issue several times in face-to-face meetings with Dow and in written comments to the EIR and EIS, but there's no response. They stonewalled.''

As I was to discover throughout my research into this case, the truth was somewhere in between. Some of the questions were unanswerable, bordering on cosmic. The Resources Agency wanted to know, for example, what growth impacts the Dow facility might have in southern California since some of Dow's products might be sold there for further processing!

Dow's consultant, Jerry Gilbert, put his finger on the real problem from Dow's point of view, when he talked about information the state agencies wanted about such secondary growth aspects. ''It would seem helpful if everyone would say, very specifically, not just we think there are growth-inducing impacts here, but describe the kind of data they want to see and the kind of assumption made . . . . The regulatory agencies and those that desire information ought to say what kind of assumptions they feel ought to be made.''

Gilbert also echoes Jones' frustrations about the search for alternative sites. ''What is the obligation of a project proponent to do statewide planning? Do you look just statewide for sites or do you expand it to include Texas and then calculate the pollution associated with transportation? The state of California never made it clear. The Brown Administration has always been very anti-planning. I told Tom Quinn he should have a state-wide air quality plan, but Quinn said there wasn't enough money. I told him the state needed an air plan because there was going to be a lot of growth. Well, the Air Board didn't do it. The Brown Administration is very ad hoc.''

On the other hand, many of the questions the state agencies asked were eminently reasonable; in fact, essential if they were to make an informed decision. As Dr. Pratt said, Dow seemed to be resisting giving out information on ethylene emissions from its facility although that gas can, in very small quantities, have serious adverse effect on tomatoes. (Remember that one of Solano County's and the Delta's top crops was tomatoes.) The agencies also wanted more detail on the potential for a chemical spill and its possible effects.

Neither Dow nor the state agencies would budge. Dow wasn't about to rewrite the EIR, but the state agencies weren't about to make any decisions without more information. In an attempt to break the impasse, Bill Press offered to hold a consolidated hearing on the permits, getting all the agencies together so that all the questions would be put on the table once and for all. Press had been recruited from the Planning and Conservation League by Governor

Brown to run his Office of Planning and Research (OPR), a think tank and operations center for the governor.

A boyish-looking, handsome man who dresses casually in the style of the Golden State, Press could pass for a California surfer if his hair wasn't turning gray. He was wearing a trendy game-warden style shirt, modish pants with button pockets back and front, and had a small leather billfold dangling from his wrist in 1979 when we met in the offices of the Sierra Club in San Francisco, where he was conferring with Club officials. He had just resigned from the OPR to direct an ill-fated statewide initiative—under the slogan "tax pig oil"—to recapture "excess" oil company profits. Press is a man with strong political ambitions.

Before joining OPR, Press led an impressively varied life, one that parallels his boss Jerry Brown's. He grew up in Delaware, got a bachelor's degree in French at Niagara University (N.Y.), and then went to the University of Fribourg in Switzerland for a master's degree in theology. He then spent nine years studying for the priesthood. "My order was the Oblates; they teach in high schools. But I decided in 1967, when I was 27, that I wanted to be more active in the community. My superiors said no; I had to make a choice. I came to the Bay Area and taught in a high school; that's all I knew how to do."[19]

Press jumped into politics, first as the manager of then-Senator Eugene McCarthy's San Francisco office in the campaign for the 1968 Democratic presidential nomination, then in several state campaigns. He worked as an aide to a state representative for several years and then headed the Planning and Conservation League (PCL), a Sacramento-based environmental and land-use organization with a moderate reputation.

Brown plucked him out of PCL. "At PCL we had written a report in 1974 that the Office of Planning and Research, which had been created in 1970, was so unused under Reagan that it should be abolished. Jerry Brown, having the fine Jesuitical mind that he does, had a different punishment in mind. So I joined OPR as deputy director in September 1975 and became director in February 1976."

Press later became a key political operative for Brown, running the day-to-day aspects of his presidential forays into Rhode Island, New Jersey, and Oregon in 1976 and his 1978 reelection as governor. But he was never a close confidant of Brown's, always operating just outside the inner circle of Tom Quinn and others. Nevertheless, Press would soon garner one of the strongest followings among California environmentalists because of his work at OPR.

Press also enjoyed a good deal of respect among businessmen throughout the state. While there was no love lost between Press and Jack Jones, Ray Brubaker, who would soon replace Al Look at Dow's Western Division, speaks highly of him. "Bill Press is a hell of a nice guy. I could talk to him and, whether he understood or not, he would at least listen." Even Richard Brann of Solano County gives Press a backhanded compliment. "Brown had visionaries on his board, and Bill Press is a visionary. But he doesn't have his feet on the ground."

Press was sorely disappointed when Dow refused his offer to hold consolidated hearings because, according to one company official, "we feared that the state just wanted to rewrite an already approved EIR." Press recounted the events for me. "Our first offer was made in March. I think it was rejected because the attitude in the company at that time was that the best strategy towards the state agencies was to divide and conquer, to take them on one at a time. They thought their chances of success were better if they were dealing with just one particular agency at one time with a given set of issues. One of the difficulties is that joint hearings are left to the prerogatives of the applicant. I remember having discussions with their consultants as well as with their own staff and strongly advising them to do so, but they chose not to." But Press doesn't point his fingers at Dow alone. "There's no doubt that the state agencies resisted those hearings just as strongly as Dow did in the beginning. They preferred to be single-purpose and narrow-minded."

I asked Press whose idea it was to hold the consolidated hearings.

> It was really my idea. I saw that as one way of cutting a lot of time and getting a decision quickly, which wouldn't be possible if the agencies didn't sit down in the same room at the same time and get the same information and make a decision simultaneously. We did hold some technical briefings for state agencies. They were very productive. They just helped clear the air. There is a great information gap with any project like this and we wanted to be sure the people in the state agencies knew the facts about the project and weren't operating on some set of assumptions they had read in the newspapers or in some environmental magazine. We wanted them to get it straight from Dow and have a chance to ask Dow any questions they might have about the project.

But why hadn't the state agencies asked these questions during the EIR process? Press is candid about what he sees as their failure to act expeditiously.

> I believe the state agencies should have responded to the original EIR.

But, in fact, until after the Dow case there was no requirement that said they had to. They knew that eventually that project was going to come to them to deal with. The blame also lies with Solano County for not consulting with the state agencies. They really didn't ask for advice. They just wanted to get it behind them. It actually would have been very unusual for a state agency to get involved at this point.

Press wasn't about to give up, however. His fallback idea was to hold what he called a "technical briefing" on the project. As head of OPR, Press had conducted a study that identified a number of problems in administering CEQA. "We found that 50 percent of the comments received by lead agencies from state agencies were really worthless and provided no significant input into the process. Another was little involvement of state agencies in the formulation or the writing of an EIR, a draft EIR, or a draft EIS. The technical briefing is one way of addressing the problem by providing more information, providing state reviewers a better perspective and a better opportunity to gather information on a major project." Press concedes that ideally the technical briefing should have been held earlier at the draft EIR stage, but says it was still useful.

If the number of people who jammed the meeting room is any indication, the briefing was a success. Almost 40 signed up to speak. Press welcomed them with a bit of the wit and good humor he displayed throughout the controversy. "I'd like to thank all of you for coming this morning and welcome you here. I am sorry about the crowded quarters. If you didn't believe this is an era of limits, now you know."

Jack Jones opened Dow's presentation and was followed by Al Gunkler. Even EIR consultant Jerry Gilbert was here—he would not appear at later hearings. State agency representatives threw questions at Dow's people and, after that, the public got its chance. But because so many people wanted to get their two cents in, the briefing did not get into much depth. It served more to introduce Dow to the state bureaucrats.

Neil Moyer of the Air Resources Board raised the most detailed issues. He wanted more information on ethylene emissions and operating figures on emissions for Dow's existing plants. Bill Press and others focused on what they thought was a rather weak analysis of secondary growth impacts in the draft EIR and asked Dow when its spill-control plan would be available. Nick Arguimbau played his gadfly role, stinging here and there. Jack Jones and others from Dow were cordial and offered to answer all questions, but the terrain was looking more like quicksand all the time.

Dow had hoped that the technical briefing would smooth ruffled feathers in the state agencies and perhaps get things moving again, but it was not to be. Claire Dedrick plunged the knife further into Dow. In June 1976, she sent a 14-page letter with eight pages of attachments to the Corps of Engineers criticizing it for failing to undertake an independent assessment of the Dow project. The Corps' EIS consisted of a 34-page summary of the project and its impacts, and a big appendix—the Gilbert-prepared EIR.

So, in Dedrick's opinion, the Corps was doing little more than regurgitating the information prepared by Dow's consultant. Dedrick went on to catalog in detail the many serious questions the state agencies still had about the project and concluded by requesting that the Corps not issue any permits until the state had resolved all of its concerns. Press' initial effort to end the stalemate thus ended in failure. Dow was, in the words of Jack Jones, "dead in the water by the summer of 1976."

The company responded by calling Ray Brubaker in from Texas to get things moving. "Brubaker arrived on the scene. He came out to build that plant. He's a builder," Jack Jones says admiringly. "He's built those things all over the world. We had every anticipation we were going to build this thing. He came in and said, 'Jesus, let's get going here.' I was under pressure from Brubaker and Midland. They wanted an up-or-down decision so they could start or wash this thing out and start somewhere else."

Beckee Beemer, who was working on getting environmental permits for Dow, had a similar impression of Brubaker. "Dow had brought in another Texan, Al Look, before Brubaker, who wanted to build big and quick. But he didn't know how to talk with the state people. I liked Ray. Jack [Jones] was good in a smoke-filled room, but not in negotiating permits like Ray."

Ray Brubaker is indeed a builder. He's an engineer who's built plants in Texas, Germany, Brazil. He has been vice president of Dow's operations in Brazil, where he was in charge of four large petrochemical complexes with 1,500 employees. Today he is back in Texas running a major facility in Freeport. He looks and sounds like someone who gets things done. Not a builder of the old school, but one who knows the new realities of putting up a plant. Bill Press characterizes Brubaker as "a real pro—very easy to deal with."

Brubaker doesn't engage in vitriol against Jerry Brown, Bill Press, the state of California, or against environmental regulations in general. "Regulations are stronger in California than in Texas or other places I've worked—and I think they need to be. People live so close together. And I don't think environmental regulations are a big competitive disadvantage for the United States. We've had to get better than we were. Things were driving us that way. We had to get more efficient instead of letting it go out the stack into the air or out a pipe into the water.''

Ray promised he would give me a straight assessment of the Dow controversy. ''I try to tell the truth because my memory isn't good enough to remember what I said.'' Like most other people from Dow, he was open and seemed eager to help identify the positive lessons to be distilled from the controversy he had been a major player in.

Brubaker says two things particularly surprised him when he came to California.

> One of them was that with all the regulations they had, they could not clearly define what they wanted and what it was you needed to answer or tell them. You'd work for months and answer all these questions and then there would be a whole new world of new questions. So that troubled me some. The other thing that was a problem, and we had not run into it anywhere else at that point, was that it was a new, grassroots site, and new sites obviously engender more emotion than expanding old sites.

Others who worked for Dow expressed similar sentiments. Beckee Beemer, who has left Dow to work for an oil company in the Bay Area, says the firm could never get a clear story from the state about just what it wanted. ''They were very nervous,'' she says, ''about a people explosion in an area with little development. But the Brown Administration never decided what it really wanted.''

Neither Press nor Brubaker was ready to give up on the Dow project, however. Press went to work within the administration to get Governor Brown to polish his image with big business. In an internal memo to Gray Davis, Brown's top aide, which was leaked to the *San Francisco Examiner* in April 1976, Press advised Brown that he had to do something about business in general and Dow in particular. With regard to Dow, Press advised the governor to ''let things take their course,'' but he also urged the agencies to ''speed up remaining permits.'' He ended the memo by counseling that ''whether Dow goes down or up, I think [it] most important that we soon give some signal of pro-business sympathy.''

The immediate reaction by some environmentalists was that Press and the governor were caving in to industry pressure. Press vigorously denies that charge, saying that his only aim was to accelerate the permit process so that industry wouldn't have to wait so long for an answer. He stresses that the governor never deviated from his avowed neutrality concerning the Dow project or his position that existing laws had to be followed.

Brubaker also swung into action. He decided to appeal Jud Callaghan's denial of air permits for the styrene plant to the independent BAAPCD hearing board, confident that Dow could persuade the board that Callaghan and Feldstein were being too tough in their interpretation of the district's regulations. "We decided to contest the BAAPCD denial and felt we could overcome that. Statewide permits were the real problem."

Brubaker and Press also agreed that things might be speeded up at the state level if Governor Brown would sit down and talk with Paul Oreffice, then head of Dow U.S.A. Brown, who had just returned from the presidential trail, agreed to such a meeting in September. Jack Jones described the scene for me.

> We arranged the meeting with Oreffice. Brubaker and I were there. Brown had all his cabinet members there. Bill Press, Claire Dedrick were there—anybody who had any policy action to make on this. We met for three hours. Brown impressed us at that time as an extremely adroit executive. He focused right away on the key questions and forced his people to give him answers. The upshot of that meeting was that Brown said my people say you won't answer all the questions and you say every time you answer one they ask 50 more and that the questions are endless or not pertinent. So let's pull all the agencies together for two days of hearings right here in Sacramento, every agency that has a state permit to give. And he turned to his people and said you give Dow a list of all the remaining questions on your minds and that's it. Those hearings will deal with those questions only. We said fine.

But why the change of heart when Dow had so recently refused Bill Press' offer to hold a consolidated hearing? "We agreed to the hearing on the basis we would get an answer quickly, yes or no," Ray Brubaker says. "That's what we really wanted. We did not want to continue working in this vacuum of no answer. So we agreed that if the hearings would speed things up and get us an answer then we would agree." So things lurched ahead for the first time in months. Dow felt it would have its answer from the state— up or down—quickly.

While Dow was negotiating over consolidated state hearings, the company also filed an appeal with the independent five-member BAAPCD hearing board on August 20, 1976. Dow asked the board to grant it the necessary air quality permits. The board had the power to override Jud Callaghan and Milton Feldstein in their interpretation of district pollution control regulations or to grant a variance to Dow if circumstances warranted.

Dow's main argument was that Callaghan and Feldstein had been overly zealous in their interpretation of district regulations, applying unreasonably tough criteria not required by any law or regulation. In a newspaper interview Jack Jones quipped, "This is the cleanest styrene plant that's ever been designed in the world. With the rules Callaghan's using, anything bigger than a gas station couldn't be built." BAAPCD's Feldstein retorted, "This case is where we decide whether air quality really means anything . . . .If economics and jobs are more important than air quality, then the law will have to be changed at the federal level."

By this time Dow's air pollution problems had attracted attention throughout the state and nation. A widely read article in *Chemical Week* observed: "The case focuses attention on the compromises that many jurisdictions are using to permit industrial growth in non-attainment areas, compromises that are sanctioned nowhere in the Clean Air Act. It underscores the confusion that prevails in the enforcement of the amendments. And it raises serious questions about growth in the nonattainment sections of California, which include the major markets and ports in San Francisco and Los Angeles areas."[20]

Representatives of the state's business community were more emotional. Peter Feary, deputy director of the business-oriented California Council for Environmental and Economic Balance, stated flatly that "if the Dow plant can't be built, then nothing can be built in a nonattainment area." Ronald Zumbrun, head of the Pacific Legal Foundation, business' "public interest" law firm, agreed. "The Dow case is a battle for the future of California's economy." Lt. Governor Mervyn Dymally, a Democratic politician with his own ambitions, chimed in, claiming a denial "would have a disastrous effect on the economy of California . . . .It will discourage other corporations from coming in."

With feelings running high, Paul DeFalco, the thoughtful, former head of EPA's regional office in San Francisco, perhaps put things in perspective best.

All the precedent isn't going to be made with Dow . . . but the case offers a good chance to test principles rather than details. The big difference in this case is that it confronts the local agency with the question of revising its rules. The Clean Air Act is a good law. It works in 90 percent of the cases, but it doesn't work where we're up against a severe nonattainment situation in an area where population and industry are growing. Congress, the Administration, and the courts have been unwilling to come to grips with the basic issue of articulating a balance between environment and economics.

Hearings were set for mid-September, but just before the battle was joined, new hope for a compromise emerged. On September 1, BAAPCD's directors convened a meeting to consider changing the infamous Section 1309 of its regulations, the one that was causing Dow such difficulty. EPA's DeFalco and the California Air Resources Board were urging the district to adopt a numerical definition of "significant" pollution by establishing a review cutoff value for each major pollutant. If the anticipated emissions fell below the cutoff value, they would be considered insignificant.

Proponents pointed out that such an approach was already in use in many other areas of the country. Dow officials felt that because their styrene plant would be super-clean, they could meet any reasonable cutoff number the district might adopt. That proposal drew cheers from the construction workers who had taken over the front-row seats in the packed hearing room, their ubiquitous posters calling for a balance between the economy and the environment.

About 40 people representing industry, labor, and local government testified in favor of the change. The following statement was typical: "The problem, simply stated, is this: EPA, the California Air Resources Board, and the Bay Area Air Pollution Control District Board, under the requirements of the Clean Air Act, are effectively taking over land-use planning and area-basing decisions on air quality alone, without regard to economic and social consequences."

While outnumbered, environmentalists were not to be outdone. They, too, pressed BAAPCD to alter its regulations but in a different way: they wanted district officials to evaluate the impact of all the units in a new facility, instead of on a piecemeal basis as was being done with Dow's petrochemical complex, by considering the cumulative emissions from all of them. The Air Resources Board also supported the environmentalists' position.

On September 15, the day before it was to present its case to the hearing board, Dow got a one-two punch to the chin. Not only did the BAAPCD's directors adopt a cumulative emissions procedure as urged by the environmentalists, but they rejected a review cutoff rule pending further study.

The next day, Dow argued its case before the hearing board. Its case was highly technical and legalistic. There would be no emotional appeal for jobs, no whining about the need to balance the social needs with air quality. William Dial, an attorney from Los Angeles whom Dow had brought in to take over from Art Shelton, had crafted a narrow appeal. He quarreled with the data and assumptions that the district officials had used in their theoretical calculations to determine if ambient air quality standards would be violated. By assuming worst case data at each point, Dial argued, BAAPCD ended up with a situation that would never happen in the real world. He also maintained that Callaghan's interpretation of the term "significant" was, in lawyers' parlance, "arbitrary and capricious," one that wasn't found in any district regulation and one that had been adopted without public hearings. Finally, Dial argued that BAAPCD was making its predictions about maximum ground-level increments of particulates at the wrong place—inside the boundaries of the site, where OSHA regulations should apply, instead of at the plant boundaries.

Given the complexity of these issues, it soon became clear the hearings would be no brief affair. In fact, the board ended up meeting practically one day a week every week during September and October just to consider the Dow application. The hearings on October 28 were typical of the jousting over technical points. At that hearing Dial called two witnesses—Conrad Miller, a Dow senior engineer, and Lewis Robinson, head of the district's research and planning section that had been responsible for evaluating Dow's application. The main thrust of Miller's testimony was that the district's method of theoretically calculating the impact of emissions from several different sources was simplistic and overestimated maximum concentrations. Miller added that more sophisticated modeling methods resulted in lower estimated concentrations.

In questioning Robinson, Dial also began to highlight inconsistencies between BAAPCD's regulations and its stated policies for the Bay Area. Robinson conceded, for example, that the agency's own air quality predictions for 1979 assumed "normal industrial growth," which included new sources of significant pollution. Dial pointed out that if the agency denied permits in cases like Dow, BAAPCD would be thwarting the growth its own predictions assumed. Robinson countered that some of the growth could take place in areas in the region that met standards and that, in any case, agency forecasts should not be regarded as the sole basis for its policies and procedures.

The hearing board adjourned on October 28, scheduling additional hearings in the near future. Jack Jones was getting edgy. He didn't like the way the Air Resources Board hearings were going. "At that time we had in the back of our minds to go to court. We thought maybe the only long-term solution was a revision of the law, but if we had to wait then a drawn-out timetable might make the whole project questionable."

Chapter 8

THE STATE HEARINGS

What do an Indian medicine man, a former Jesuit, a Texan industrialist, and the head of the Ecobalance Planning Committee have in common? They were all players in the formal hearing set up by Bill Press to consider the Dow project. The hearings would turn into a monumental, often dramatic, affair.

While hearing transcripts aren't the best of bedtime reading, wading through more than 1,000 pages of testimony and an equal number of pages of written statements was well worth it. The essence of the dispute is here. Like the skin of an onion, as one layer is peeled away, another emerges: complex issues and no easy answers. Industry versus environmentalists. Environmentalists versus the state agencies. The state agencies versus industry. Thoughtful, penetrating questions and answers interspersed with wild and silly claims by both sides.

And through it all is an uneasy sense of uncertainty among everyone, like canoeing a river for the first time and not being able to scout the rapids around the bend even though you can hear the roar. Bad enough when you're wearing a life preserver and all you really risk is a dunking or at worst a lost boat, more nerve-wracking by far when jobs, prosperity, human health, and the future of the Pacific Flyway are on the line. Here was the dilemma of a modern society trying to make a decision with so much knowledge and yet not enough. We are all taught not to act without all the facts before us, but the result seems to be a loss of nerve, a creeping paralysis. Getting more information was one of the key goals of the consolidated hearings.

As Governor Brown had ordered, the state agencies submitted a list of 74 detailed questions to Dow on November 5, 1976, and Dow started spending money to get some more answers. The questions were broad and varied: What about air pollution transport into the San Joaquin Valley? What about salt water intrusion up the Sacramento? What about an oil spill in the Suisun Marsh? Dow was to have answers in time for two days of hearings in December. "I spent $300,000 getting the data to answer those questions. [We went to] not just Dow people, but outside experts, like Stanford Research Institute," Jack Jones asserts.

Jones says Dow was reasonably optimistic because some tight ground rules for conducting the hearings had been agreed to by Governor Brown and Bill Press.

> This was going to be, basically, strictly a technical session. We also said to add responsibility to this, so you don't have somebody walking off the street making wild speculative statements for which they have no education or qualification to comment on, that people who were going to testify at this hearing would have to give two weeks advance notice and state their qualifications. And the testimony would be sworn testimony, taken under oath in an effort to add responsibility to the statements so that a lot of the slanderous things could perhaps be toned down. We said fine. I brought 15 witnesses to the hearings and submitted all the information in advance.

The preparations for the meeting made by Bill Press, his staff, and state agency people were likewise impressive. They assembled a 60-page briefing book for participants and the public. It set out what promised to be an exhausting two-day schedule. Specific topics were enumerated for each session and witnesses listed. The major issues would be air and water quality, hazardous waste disposal, public health, economic effects, and the cumulative impact of the project. The briefing book summarized these issues and included an annotated list of the questions that Dow had been asked by the state agencies to answer.

Bill Press would act as convenor for the joint hearings, but each session would be chaired by a representative of one of the permitting agencies or boards. In this way, the consolidated hearings would satisfy any statutory hearing requirements that a particular agency or board had to meet before issuing Dow a permit. The permitting agencies, from which Dow needed a total of nine permits, would listen to testimony, but would not actually take any votes at the hearing. Permit decisions would be made independently by each agency or board after the hearings closed.

The hearings opened a few minutes late on the morning of December 8, 1976. The room was jammed as Press convened the meeting. The whole cast of characters was there, from Ray Brubaker to Nick Arguimbau and from Cynthia Kay to Richard Brann—politicians, businessmen, environmentalists, public officials, and concerned citizens. Bill Press opened with these remarks: "This is, in fact, an historic moment, for it represents the first time that two or more state agencies have sat together to consider a major development permit.'' Press went on to discuss the significant advantages in the process he saw for both industry and environmentalists. ''First, it telescopes the long hearing process by combining several hearings into one, thereby saving a great deal of time and money for the developer, for the reviewing agencies, and for the general public. Second, and just as importantly, it provides for the decision makers a more complete overview of a complex proposal such as this one. The result, we are convinced, will be better for environmentally sound decisions.''

So far, so good, Jack Jones remembers thinking. But then, claims Jones, Press dropped a bombshell that changed the rules of the game, in effect double-crossing Dow.

> As the meeting opened we were advised by Bill Press—he was sort of the hearing officer—that the requirement that witnesses give two weeks' advance notice was being waived, their qualifications were being waived, and there would not be sworn testimony, but they would be asked to promise to tell the truth. Press said he felt they couldn't deny anyone the chance to testify if they appeared. Further, Press announced he had a letter from the attorney general that had been written by Larry King two days before—it wasn't known to us until that morning—in which he advised Senator Dunlap, who was from that district and had some concern about the project, that the proceedings that were about to take place would have to be treated as a supplemental environmental impact report. That put us back to ground zero because we'd have to go through all the massaging, the hearings, and the protest periods again.

Bill Press recounts a different version. ''I never said that only Dow could testify. That was legally impossible. We were told that we couldn't legally prevent any member of the public from testifying simply because they hadn't signed up beforehand. These people were put under oath—made to swear to tell the truth.'' Press does concede that the letter was a surprise, and that Dow was going to face further delay, but says neither he nor the governor had any control over that. ''There was a newspaper article in the *Oakland Tribune*. They called it the letter that broke Dow's back.''

Larry King explained to me why the letter was written and why it was important.

> One of the legislators asked for some advice and we decided we'd make it to the five agencies instead. I wrote what we called an informal letter of advice. I probably should have mounted it because I went through

an enjoyable session with the witch-hunt after Dow left at which that opinion letter was notorious.

[It was] a typical governmental opinion letter, though. It gave our clients three options to go through. Didn't really state a whole lot. It had in it some of the historical facts, footnotes galore that had a lot of meat to them, warnings about what could be some of the problems. But basically it gave three options regarding the EIR: If you like it, go ahead and use it. If you use it and it's not adequate, your whole permit process will be null and void and the court will set aside your decision. Two, supplement the EIR yourself if you don't think it's adequate. Three, there's a federal EIS that you may join in and produce a joint document.

That's where the agencies, I think, were headed but that was going to be more of a nightmare than it was going to be a help and I think just before Dow said let's go away, the agencies had already started drafting a joint powers agreement with the Corps.

What exactly did the letter mean in terms of the way the hearing would be run? Bill Press explained to the crowd:

The California attorney general ruled only yesterday that state agencies must concur in the adequacy of an EIR before acting on a permit application and may submit an inadequate EIR to the EIR process where necessary to do so. Consequently, a further important purpose of this hearing is to permit state agencies to comply with CEQA by gathering whatever additional information may be necessary to formally supplement the Dow EIR compliance with CEQA and with yesterday's attorney general's ruling. It will require additional time; it will require compilation of a transcript of this hearing and other supplemental materials into a supplemental EIR document. It will also require circulating that document for public and government agency comment through the state clearinghouse [a process used in most states whereby major projects are reviewed for their fiscal, environmental, and other impacts], but this is a requirement and a responsibility that state agencies will comply with.

Thus, the letter that King characterized as advisory was elevated to a ruling. As one state official later observed, "King positioned himself so that he was advising state agencies as 'clients' even though none of them were. More importantly, state agencies were *taking* his advice as if it was binding."

Although Dow didn't object or protest when the King letter was introduced, Jones says they were outraged. But later Jones told me that he didn't think King was out to get Dow. "Larry King's purpose at the time, I suspect, was to try to put the hearings into a posture that would make it immune from legal assault. He thought there would be more legal suits filed as a result of this very unusual

procedure. There was no procedure for doing this. You were just
making the rules as you went along and being mindful that all these
environmental law suits had been determined on procedural grounds
and not on substantive environmental concerns. I think he was trying
to be helpful in that respect.'' Bill Press says the letter set the tone
for the day—highly emotional. ''It was a packed house and everyone
was disgruntled.''

Press turned the meeting over to Ken Cory, chairman of the
California Lands Commission, who had to give Dow permission to
use state property for the project. Art Shelton was back on the scene,
coordinating Dow's presentation. He introduced Al Gunkler as Dow's
first witness. Gunkler gave the audience a general overview of the
project. He took a very practical approach, pointing out all the
various everyday products that were derived from the chemicals
Dow would produce: polyethylene—plastic food wrapping and elec-
trical insulation; styrene—plastic for containers and home insulation;
vinyl chloride—upholstery, records, pipes, and kitchen floors. Gunkler
stressed Dow's established record in environmental protection, pointing
to the awards his company had won. He emphasized all the jobs
the complex would create and explained that the project would save
energy and cut prices for West Coast consumers. Finally, Gunkler
made it clear that Dow needed to build the entire complex—it would
not make economic sense to build only the styrene plant.

Cory, Bill Press, and others on the hearing panel started to probe,
but their questioning was tentative. Cory wanted to know where
Dow would get all the power (170 megawatts) it was going to need
for the complex. Gunkler said Dow had not yet made a decision
on how it was going to meet its energy needs. Cory also wanted to
know how diligent Dow had been in negotiating with U.S. Steel to
purchase land in Pittsburg. Gunkler replied that Dow had a letter
dated August 1974 in which U.S. Steel said they were holding it
for future steel production. Another question was asked about Dow's
oil spill record at Pittsburg. Gunkler parried that one, saying that
in 40 years there had only been one spill—50 gallons of styrene—
and it was quickly contained. These three issues would surface again
and again, but for now Gunkler was off the hook.

Robert Perry, a Dow engineer who coordinated the overall project,
was next to testify. He showed slides while discussing the land-use
and water quality impacts of the project. He touched on the Williamson Act contract, noting the large cancellation fee Dow paid,
and discussed Solano County's new industrial plan for Collinsville
that was in the works. Water quality, Perry maintained, wouldn't

be any problem at all. "None of the effects on salinity would be measurable. They are so small that you wouldn't be able to measure them in the Delta anyway." The same was true, Perry suggested, with respect to the dredging associated with the dock, turning basin, and pipelines.

Again the questioning was brief. The issue of oil spills and shipping hazards cropped up again, and two of the panel members wanted to know more about where Dow was going to dispose of the 2,000-5,000 barrels of toxic wastes the complex would produce each year. Perry said Dow would cover that issue later in the hearings.

Cory also expressed concerns about the impact of dredging on fish and wildlife in the area and the possibility that the U.S. Army Corps of Engineers might have complete and preemptive authority since the Sacramento River was a navigable waterway. "I want to know what Dow's position would be, whether or not they would continue as good citizens to conform to [California Commission on] Fish and Game's regulations, or would [they] hide behind the federal Corps regulation. And what I am wanting you to do is, in essence, waive a right. This will be cold turkey. There are a lot of people in this state [for whom this] is a very important issue." Perry didn't hesitate in replying: "Dow would, I am sure, meet the requirements and work with Fish and Game. Fish and Game has been very reasonable in their suggestions and very reasonable requirements. And Dow would voluntarily follow what Fish and Game has offered."

By now, Dow was running behind time in its presentation and several politicians were waiting to say their piece. Dow deferred to them, and with good reason—each wanted the project built. State Sen. John Nejedly, author of the Suisun Preservation Act and a representative from the Pittsburg area, said he supported Dow because of high unemployment. But to him, it was "this whole picture that concerns me more than the specifics of this case." Nejedly recounted what he said were unwarranted hurdles Dow had faced and outlined legislation he would propose, based on the consolidated hearings, to make the system work better by getting all questions on the table early. Bill Press agreed with Nejedly: " . . . the whole issue here today is not the Dow project in particular, but the general problem of the development of an approval process. I don't think it has to take so much time. I don't think it has to take so much paperwork. I don't think it has to cost so much money."

Assemblyman John Knox voiced similar sentiments. Knox, who authored the California Environmental Quality Act of 1970 and the law that made the San Francisco Bay Conservation Commission a permanent agency, lamented that "one of the great tragedies here with respect to the Dow application is we are having single-purpose hearings all around the Bay Area. We have one group that's worried only about the air and one group will discuss the water, and somebody else will discuss transportation, and somebody else will discuss solid waste, and so on and so on. And each discipline makes its decision based on its own concern and somehow the basic and overall concern of the public gets lost in the cracks . . . . We have to balance. Every time a house is built we have to balance what effect it has on the environment."

Assemblyman Dan Boatwright, chairman of the powerful Ways and Means Committee in the California Assembly that controlled the budget of the Resources Agency, came on much stronger. Boatwright, a real estate developer from Contra Costa County, had authored the state's Native Species Wildlife and Conservation Act, and was the only legislator to have received the Sierra Club's Wildlife Conservationist of the Year award. Boatwright felt strongly, too, about the Suisun Marsh. "I might say that I also hunt ducks there. I hunted last Saturday there. It wasn't a good day; it was kind of still, but nevertheless, that's where I hunt. That's where I go to work to clean out the ditches and cut the tules back without burning, and it's vital that we preserve the Suisun Marsh. And I work to preserve it."

But Boatwright was just warming up; he hadn't come to trade pleasantries. He lectured the panel on California's bad business image and the high unemployment rate in his district—21 percent in Pittsburg alone. He cited testimony his committee had heard from a bank economist who predicted California would have an unemployment rate of 18 percent by 1980. He concluded with a thinly veiled warning to the state agencies present:

In closing, just let me state that other legislators . . . are concerned about the Dow plant. Not for the Dow plant itself, but in terms of jobs and how business throughout the United States is viewing this application. Over two years, $10 million spent, 65 required permits, two granted, from 19 agencies. This is a nightmare and I want to tell you something. The California legislature is not going to stand still for this. We are working on bills right now, including one as a backup bill, that will state something to the effect, notwithstanding all other provisions of law, the Dow plan as proposed, et cetera, is hereby authorized. Now, you may not like that, but let me tell you something. Let me tell you what the real endangered species is in California—the working man.

Tension was high after Boatwright's fiery oratory, but things cooled down a bit as Robert Perry resumed testifying, discussing the various and sundry permits and approvals Dow would need for the 13-unit facility. He noted that Dow had already secured a few approvals. Three easement agreements had been signed with the California Department of Fish and Game covering the pipeline crossings, Sherman Island and the Sacramento-San Joaquin Rivers, the turning basin, and the water permit. Perry also reported that a water pollution discharge permit had been granted by the Central Region of the California Water Quality Control Board contingent upon final approval of the EIR. That permit also carried conditions dealing with salinity.

Under questioning by Bill Press, Perry likewise described permits and approvals yet to be secured from BAAPCD and from Solano and Contra Costa counties. Press also asked if Dow wouldn't need a permit from the state Energy Commission, since they would be generating over 100 megawatts of electricity. Perry said no single unit would be that big, but conceded that Dow was hazy as to "just how it would be done." He mentioned the possibility of using geothermal power. Perry acknowledged that there was no implied state approval of Dow's energy plans and that the company was assuming a business risk in proceeding.

Ray Brubaker took the stand next in an attempt to satisfy the panel on the energy question. He detailed Dow's interest in geothermal power and related that the company had dropped its interest in financing several small dams when it learned the state wasn't happy with that idea. Brubaker also pointed out that it would be possible to efficiently generate power from a gas turbine or jet engine as was already done at Dow's Pittsburg plant.

Cory and others continued to press Brubaker for more information, asking that additional data be submitted after the hearings. Brubaker became a little testy, his impatience showing through when he was asked, as Al Gunkler had been earlier, if the styrene plant could stand by itself. "Quite frankly," Brubaker replied, "it's not our intention to start down that track until the people of the state of California, its various elected officials, and its various appointed officials indicate to us that that's what they want. No, that's not a promise. It's not anything. It's just saying that if the people of California don't want us here, we are not going to try to get under some quirk of the law because the law can be changed." That exchange brought the morning meeting to a close.

The afternoon session, chaired by John Bryson of the California

Water Resources Control Board, opened with a brief recap of Dow's energy requirements by Robert Perry. The rest of that session was a grab bag. Clayne Munk, planning director of Solano County, defended the county's planning record and, specifically, the handling of the Dow project. He asserted that these hearings weren't going to be very useful. "These studies [for the EIR] took place a year and a half ago and our hearings approximately a year ago. I have not, during this period of time, heard of brand new subjects which were not identified in the Environmental Impact Report." He pleaded with the panel to consider local wishes. "We believe that local government should also have some input and say into land use within its own county so that there are others besides individual interests or state agencies."

But Munk stumbled a bit when he was pressed on the question of whether the county's master plan contemplated industrial development on the McOmie ranch. Even though Munk claimed the 1967 plan indicated such development, he had a hard time explaining why then the county had entered into a Williamson Act contract on it: " . . . our general plan, it's somewhat general in nature, and in the southeast plan in the text as well as the diagram map, it indicated that in this general area industry is needed, and wanted, and so shown. It could have been an adjacent property, one under a contract or one that was not—I don't have an agriculture preserve map with me at this moment. But we do not find it inconsistent that land be placed in the agriculture preserve and then five years down the road, after the contract has been entered into, to find that an industry desires that particular section of property."

Munk also had trouble answering a penetrating question from Bill Press. Munk claimed that the county-approved EIR had been an exhaustive document. But why, then, Press wanted to know, had Dow followed up with a comprehensive marine spill assessment study and why had the county hired consultants to prepare a detailed land-use industrialization plan for the Collinsville area after the fact. "I'm sure we had enough information," Munk replied. "As far as the Dow proposal itself, we were asked, as far as staff and also our Commission, Board of Supervisors, that all the issues had been raised—there was nothing significant that could not be mitigated successfully . . . ."

When Press finished, Robert Pratt of the California Department of Food and Agriculture grilled Munk further about the Williamson Act cancellation and its implications for future industrial intrusion into the Montezuma Hills. Munk came back strong: "Well, let me point something out. You will not find a county anywhere in the state that is a greater friend to agriculture than Solano County. I don't care what that county is. Solano County has befriended agriculture right down the line. Let me give you a couple of examples. Ninety-two percent of all people in Solano County—and there are 190,000 of us—92 percent live in the cities, less than 8 percent live in the unincorporated area. Our county is not saturated with special service districts. We are not providing houses helter-skelter by way of districts and you find that, on the contrary, that's a unique situation.''

Pratt continued sparring with Munk until Bill Press intervened. How much of this land was prime agricultural, Press asked Pratt. Practically none, Pratt admitted. What was presently grown on the little sliver of prime land along the river? Nothing, Pratt conceded. Press drove home his point. "Well, the problem I have, if this land over here is prime, is not being farmed, and what is being farmed is not prime but marginal land at best, not returning more than $70 an acre in light of the state's agricultural economic interest, what difference is it going to make if that site is in industry or barley?'' Pratt replied what he feared, aside from air quality problems, was a "Rhineland developing up the Sacramento River, one plant after another.'' But he had to concede that "the agricultural value of that site is not high.''

Clayne Munk also got moral support from the next witness, Anthony Dehaesas, the planning director of Contra Costa County. Dehaesas read a long resolution passed by the County Planning Commission endorsing the project. In short, Dehaesas said Contra Costa County was happy with Solano's work. He made one particularly important point—although the most serious environmental problems in Contra Costa County were linked with existing plants, no one seemed to be doing much about them.

So far testimony and questioning had pretty much stuck to technical questions and specifics of the Dow project, except for the triumvirate of politicians who had urged approval. Jack Jones had worried there would be a lot of irresponsible allegations from environmentalists. Ironically, the most egregious claims would come from some of the project's proponents, particularly labor types. The first was Peter Muller of the East Bay District Associated General Contractors of California. Muller, who ran a contracting business, was also a founding member of COLAB, an anti-environmentalist labor and business coalition.

Muller started off on an even keel, detailing Contra Costa County's unemployment woes, which were hobbling an affirmative action program he was heading. He pleaded for balance between the economy and environment, and complimented the state for holding the consolidated hearings. But then he cited the Fantus study (Fantus is a national firm specializing in plant location consulting) that ranked California at the bottom of the seven western states in business climate. That got Bill Press' hackles up:

> I would like to remark for the purposes of this hearing that report does not in any way address environmental regulations and the need for that in determining positive or negative business climate. And, secondly, to remark that that report also concluded that the state's ranking, so far as business climate is concerned, is one of the least important factors in industry's mind when they make a decision whether or not to locate in a particular state. There are many more factors that are considered, and I think I would invite you to go back to that point that may have escaped your attention the first time around.

Later the evening of December 8, 1976, other labor and business representatives would sound a refrain similar to Muller's. Doyle Williams of the local steamfitters union and spokesman for COLAB, made an impassioned plea for jobs:

> It's very easy for me to stand before you and say, stop Dow Chemical, stop freeway construction, stop the deep waterport construction, when I'm on a 52-week salary job yearly. But there are a lot of other people out in this audience today that are not on a 52-week a year salary and are on seasonal employment. We can't bring about an environmentally pure atmosphere overnight without destroying the fiber of our economy . . . .Contra Costa, Solano, and Napa building trades are going through a 20 to 30 percent unemployment rate. Our own local union, Steamfitters Local 342, has 1,250 active members involved in it and . . . we are approaching 600 unemployed, 48 percent.

John Bryson of the Water Resources Control Board agreed with Williams that unemployment was a problem, but reminded him that sewage treatment projects, which had been pushed by environmentalists, were providing thousands of construction jobs across the nation. And Bill Press got Williams to admit that by Dow's own calculations the project would provide only 170 jobs for pipefitters during the peak construction period. Yet Williams persisted. "Well, I can only say this, Mr. Press, that if the Dow Chemical plant doesn't go and/or if the standards of the Bay Area Air Pollution [Control District] aren't lowered in some way to allow new industry to build, there simply won't be any new industry built. I can't very well blame new industry for not coming into the area.''

Billie Bowes, representing the California Coordinating Council, a coalition of 35 labor and business coalitions, was even more vociferous. She claimed California was "fast becoming a disaster state where no company wishes to invest capital. If we lose this Dow project . . . we will have announced to the whole world that California will no longer be a place to invest or work or live.'' Bowes ended by castigating environmentalists. "I ask you to insist that those who make wild claims provide you with proof of their statements. Make them prove how the Dow plant will destroy our environment. I'm tired of scare stories and innuendoes.''

But Bowes had made a few wild claims of her own. She maintained the Dow facility was so clean that it would put out less "air pollution than 22 cars driving 50 miles an hour.'' Bill Press pounced on that like a cat. "I would ask you to provide proof of your statement that this complex of 13 plants, which is going to emit 1.8 tons of hydrocarbons and 11.1 tons of nitrous oxide and 1.8 tons of sulfur dioxide and 2.5 tons of particulates per day is emitting less than 22 cars . . . .'' Bowes quickly started backing down, saying she didn't know the hearing was on all 13 plants and that she was talking about the styrene plant only. Press pressed harder—where did she get her information? Bowes admitted she had asked Dow to prepare it for her. Press turned to Al Gunkler of Dow who said they meant only hydrocarbons from the styrene plant when referring to 22 cars.

The love-in between labor and Dow was shaken a bit, however, by Rex Cook, secretary-treasurer of the local Oil, Chemical, and Atomic Workers International Union. Cook rose to say that his union, whose members work inside oil refineries, chemical plants, and the like, opposed any reduction in standards or regulations just to accommodate Dow. Cook voiced his concern about what he said was the higher incidence of certain cancers in heavily industrialized Contra Costa County compared to the nation as a whole, California, or the Bay Area. He also asked if Dow could guarantee that the community would not be exposed to vinyl chloride emissions from the proposed facility. Cook closed by questioning Dow's track record in the area of occupational health, accusing the company of using its own workers as guinea pigs in studying the effects of vinyl chloride.

Cook's testimony stood in stark contrast to that of his labor brethren. Were he and his union singularly enlightened or was there something more behind it? Apparently there was. First, Dow's anti-union reputation was well-known. While it would contract with unionized construction firms, once the plant was built, Dow would do everything possible to keep Cook and his union out. Cook's union thus faced the prospect of a bitter organizing battle with a big, well-heeled company during a time of high unemployment. There was also a history of bad blood between the Oil, Chemical and Atomic Workers and the Building Trades Council.

Tony Canada of the Contra Costa Central Labor Council, which covered many workers in the construction industry, asserted that Cook was just trying to get back at Canada's people who had the most to gain if the project went through. Canada accused Cook of hypocrisy: "I spent some 29 years as a steelworker. It's my feeling, as Mr. Rex has pointed out to you, I would do the utmost to walk every one of the steelworkers out of U.S. Steel if it was polluting. I mean, clean your own home first is what I'm trying to say. Everyone knows that Shell and some of the other plants which he represents are the biggest polluters in the state of California. If I felt as strongly as he does, I would lead my membership out of the plant and say, 'Let's leave here because we are polluting, we are hurting the environment.' "

Like labor, environmentalists were generally of one mind about the project, only they were against it. For the most part, the major environmental groups like the Sierra Club and Friends of the Earth stuck to specific substantive objections they had to the project—the Williamson Act cancellation, the faulty EIR, the air pollution problem. That's not to say they didn't engage in a bit of hyperbole of their own or go cosmic at times in what some might characterize as classic California style. And they certainly made it clear there would be no compromise. The Clean Air Act was plain in what it said and environmentalists didn't like the idea of offsets to accommodate new growth if it meant a delay in achieving air quality standards. No matter that the land was producing only $70 per acre per year in crops and meat, it was going to be kept in open space. But, by and large, the histrionics were left to what Jack Jones refers to as the "lunatic fringe," those who would later turn the hearings into a sideshow the evening of the second day of the hearings.

Nick Arguimbau led off for the environmentalists, briefly summarizing the many questions he had about the project. He claimed that in breaking the Williamson Act contract on the McOmie Ranch, Dow was taking more land out of protection than had been done during the first four years of the act's existence. He asked whether there had been adequate consideration of the impact of vinyl chloride production and whether the state really wanted such a capital-intensive, polluting industry given the concern over jobs and clean air. Arguimbau also criticized the hearing because there was nothing specific on the agenda about the California Lands Commission's responsibility to preserve state property along the Sacramento River that had been designated environmentally significant. And he questioned whether the hearings were going to be of any use in rectifying any problems in an inadequate EIR. When Arguimbau was through, the message was clear to all that the hearings would be longer and probably more difficult than either Dow or the state had contemplated.

The last two hours of the afternoon session were given over to Dow to address air quality issues in greater detail. By now, however, the hearings were running several hours behind schedule, so Dow eliminated two of its speakers, experts on dispersion of air contaminants and the effects of air pollution on agriculture. These subjects would, according to Art Shelton, be covered by other speakers.

Before introducing Bill Beamer, who would discuss air emissions from the facility, Shelton took a swipe at Nick Arguimbau.

> One of the problems that we have run into is a general understanding in the community—that we cannot reach—that there will be a disaster if this is built. And quite the opposite is true . . . .One illustration of that: Even the man here from the Sierra Club [Arguimbau] quoted to you a figure stating that this proposed facility would manufacture something like 30 percent of the total vinyl chloride monomer required in the United States. Now, he knows that isn't true. He knows that the total production of this proposed facility is less than 10 percent of the amount required nationally and an amount designed to service only a part of the existing western market. We have trouble with these factual things. So I earnestly ask you to pay attention to this next series of witnesses.

Beamer, a Ph.D. chemist who had been with Dow for 30 years, addressed air pollution aspects of the facility. He focused on the impact the complex would have on the surrounding area and concluded that, based on Dow's calculations, there would not be any significant effect.

Tom Austin of the Air Resources Board, who was advising other state agencies on air pollution matters, followed. He agreed with Dow that the styrene plant would be "cleaner than most petrochemical complexes that we are familiar with," but emphasized that wasn't the real issue. The San Francisco area already had serious air pollution problems; it needed to reduce existing hydrocarbon emissions by 400 tons per day to meet current state standards and help reduce smog that plagued the region. The same was true of several other pollutants. Thus, even though the styrene plant was clean, the complex was going to cause air quality problems. "The 13-facility complex would [emit] 1.8 tons [of hydrocarbons] per day, a substantially greater number and far in excess of any new source review rule cutoff that we think would be acceptable to the Environmental Protection Agency . . . .Comparing those [nitrous oxide] emissions to other large industrial sources in the Bay Area, this would also show up as being a very significant NOX contributor. Emissions would be as large or larger than many refineries. It's not a small source."

But Austin agreed with Dow that BAAPCD's review rule for new sources of air pollution had problems, criticizing it as inflexible. Even if there was some sort of offset policy, however, Austin said that while Dow might be able to reduce emissions at Pittsburg sufficiently to trade off the increases associated with the styrene plant, he questioned whether it could squeeze out enough offsets to mitigate emissions from the other 12 units. One way to mitigate these emissions, Austin suggested, was for Dow to negotiate with the oil refineries in the areas that would supply Dow with naptha to reduce emissions from their facilities. He also floated the idea that Dow might consider reducing its large nitrous oxide emissions, attributable largely to Dow's proposed 175-megawatt gas turbine generator, as a trade-off against its significant hydrocarbon emissions, even though the air in the Bay Area did not violate nitrous oxide standards. This would be permissible, he explained, because nitrous oxide and hydrocarbons both contributed to smog.

Art Shelton introduced Dow's next witness, Dr. Warren Johnson, who was with EPA before joining the Stanford Research Institute. Dow had hired Johnson to study the proposed facility's air impact, especially downwind in the Sacramento and San Joaquin valleys. Perhaps cognizant of the controversy about Jerry Gilbert and the EIR, Johnson was quick to stress he had been completely independent in his work and had had "minimal interaction" with Dow during the study.

Johnson had used a detailed, sophisticated computer model to simulate where air pollution from the complex would go. He concluded, contrary to what most people believed, that due to wind direction and terrain, there would be no transport of air pollution towards Sacramento during the smog season. It would go, instead, towards Stockton. Even then, Johnson said, most of the pollution would be so diluted by the time it had gone just a few miles from the plant that there was nothing to worry about.

Indeed, Johnson asserted that the emissions from the plant would actually lead to a decrease in the area's ozone because the plant's substantial nitrous oxide emissions would react with the ozone and destroy it. He did qualify that claim by saying that if another large hydrocarbon source were built in the area (such as a PG&E power plant or an ARCO chemical complex), things might be worse since there would be more hydrocarbons for the nitrous oxide to react with.

Tom Austin of the ARB couldn't believe his ears. He conceded that there could be a short-term ozone benefit from the Dow emissions, but that Johnson's model couldn't be used to predict what would happen 10-12 hours later or in the long term, especially in the Central Valley. At the time, the ARB was conducting its own study of air pollution transport from the Bay Area, but it wasn't ready yet and Austin didn't get a chance to pursue the matter in greater depth.

The hearings were falling further behind schedule, in large part because Dow's presentations were running longer than expected. But many people who had come to Sacramento to have their say expected to be heard. That meant the rest of the afternoon and all of the evening session would have to turn to public comments. The public comment sessions, open to anyone who wanted to speak, lacked any real focus. Some of the statements were reasoned and thoughtful; others histrionic. Neither opponents nor proponents had a corner on rationality or diatribe. Both the California League of Women Voters and the California Lung Association, hardly "ultra-extremist, no-growth environmentalists," came out strongly against the project on air quality grounds. A covey of protestors from the Sacramento-Davis area, including the Sacramento County government, area farmers, and students, voiced similar sentiments. However, none could come up with any solid evidence to discount Johnson's assertion that Sacramento wouldn't be bothered by air pollution from the project during the smog season.

A Contra Costa County resident, Ellen Widess, a professor at the University of California who consulted with Friends of the Earth on land-use issues, criticized Solano County, particularly its handling of the EIR. Joseph Brecher, who was representing the Sierra Club and Friends of the Earth in the Dow BAAPCD appeal, emphasized Dow's air pollution problems. Brecher alleged that any time Dow ran into trouble with the amount of pollutants the facility would spew out, it simply changed the figures to suit its argument—

what Brecher called a "corporate tap dance." He also claimed that if Dow didn't like what its expert said, it simply went out and hired another until it heard what it wanted. Jack Jones and others from Dow steamed at that suggestion, but wouldn't get a chance to answer until the next day.

Brecher also spit some venom towards Bill Press when Press suggested that there might be something in Dow's argument that OSHA rather than California or EPA standards should apply within the plant boundaries. "Mr. Press, if that's your attitude, then you are suggesting that in this country we do have a license to pollute. A rich polluter can buy up as much private land around his plant as he needs to make sure that he will get in no matter how much pollution he emits."

Brecher also rebuked Press for insisting that environmental groups substantiate their claims regarding air pollution. He said BAAPCD had plenty of information and, in any case, Press had things backwards. The environmentalists had made a prima facie case that standards were being violated and now it was up to the agencies, with their large staffs, to do the work: "Now, Friends of the Earth and the Sierra Club have neither the time, the money, the staff, nor the expertise to examine in detail the massive submission Dow has submitted . . . .Don't ask us to produce the information because we don't have the facilities. We are volunteers and we don't have the expertise." Brecher concluded by saying that the Sierra Club and other environmentalists were strongly opposed to the trade-off policy being bandied about until existing air quality standards were met. "We should not let existing big-time corporate polluters use up the air resources of our area."

But there were an equal number of people in favor of the project. Besides Tony Canada, Doyle Williams and Billie Bowes, a host of other supporters came from the ranks of labor and business. The president of the 1.5 million member California Labor Federation, AFL-CIO, warned that unemployment among the young was a time bomb. The Independent Construction Contractors of Contra Costa County voiced similar sentiments. Greg Linde of the Southern Pacific Land Company, which owned land just downstream from the proposed Dow complex, claimed there was not another suitable site for petrochemical production in all of California. He added that there was already a pervasive feeling among plant site investigators that California was not a good place in which to do business.

All in all, the panel heard from 47 witnesses on December 8, 1976, before adjourning around 11 P.M. Everyone was exhausted and many were mad, too. Bill Press remembers: "After the first day, environmentalists had marched down to the Attorney General's office and filed a complaint claiming Dow was getting more than its fair share of time to present its case and that we were handling them roughly and unfairly when they were giving testimony. Dow complained too that it was getting short shrift and that the rules of the game had been changed."

In an attempt to give everyone more time, Press and his fellow panel members decided to extend the hearings to a third day. Dow agreed to defer the remainder of its testimony on air pollution until December 17 and to make the rest of its technical presentation now.

Dr. Jack Kilian, Dow's director of occupational health and medical research, talked first, discussing at length the issue of pollution and public health, and concentrating on community concerns about cancer. He candidly stated that this was a very difficult presentation for him to make because "there is a wealth of conflicting opinions, but only meager facts upon which one can draw a reasonable scientific conclusion." The questions Kilian asked made it obvious that the panel and many in the audience were particularly concerned with the health effects on workers, particularly those of vinyl chloride, even though none of the state agencies had any jurisdiction over occupational health.

Gordon Edlin, a professor of genetics at the University of California/Davis, who had formerly worked for Standard Oil, blasted Dow's testing of workers exposed to vinyl chloride and pointed out that Dow alone among big chemical producers was still fighting implementation of the national Toxic Substances Control Act. Barbara Des Rochers of Friends of the Earth also talked emotionally about the dangers of vinyl chloride. She wanted alarms installed throughout the complex and in the surrounding communities that would sound if vinyl chloride concentrations reached an excessive level.

E.C. Carlson was next for Dow. He discussed water quality impacts of the project, which he said, confidently, would be no problem. He was emphatic that there would be no observable effect on the salinity of the Sacramento attributable to Dow's withdrawing water.

There was some quibbling over whether Dow's pipelines and plants would be built to meet the state's tough seismic standards. Art Shelton got hot and stated flatly that Dow knew what maximum quake level it had to design for and that it "would not undertake any more detailed studies in connection with this permit process.

It is not required by law. The problems are identified, the techniques are there . . . .No person in this world can be expected to do all the detailed design engineering before it knows whether or not it's getting permits. Detailed design engineering runs to about 7 percent of the total project cost. That would be $35 million. There is no corporation in the world that I know of that would do that in advance of the permit procedure.''

But Pete Stromberg of the California Seismic Safety Commission indicated that a liquefied natural gas (LNG) terminal being built in central California had to come up with detailed designs before the EIR had been certified for that project; the implication being that if the state wanted more information, it would not hesitate to ask for it.

The panel then turned to another key water quality issue—the potential adverse effects of any spills of hazardous materials into the Sacramento River. Stephen Moore, representing the Sierra Club, made his case before Dow because he was not able to stay for the afternoon session. Moore, a private consultant hired by Larry Silver, had a good deal of experience in assessing the effects of oil spills on marine ecosystems.[21] Moore criticized Dow's EIR. He stated that while the EIR did acknowledge that accidental spills were possible and that it identified potential problems associated with them, he concluded that the ''discussion is cursory at best. The effects of certain materials on specific organisms and habitats are briefly mentioned. No attempt is made in the EIR to describe specific hypothetical scenarios which realistically represent potential spills.''

Moore did acknowledge that Dow's new spill assessment plan, which had been made public only two days earlier, remedied these defects in some respects, but he still saw some serious holes in it based on a quick review. His most serious criticism was that the maximum spill Dow assumed was way too small. He also said more information was needed on the composition of the naptha Dow would use since naptha contained substances that varied greatly in water solubility. His final barb was that most of the data Dow relied on were pre-1973 in origin when much more recent, reliable information was available.

Dow got its chance to respond to Moore that afternoon. Bob Perry stressed that Dow had an exemplary record in this area—only one small spill ever. Moreover, Perry asserted the spill plan, which cost $200,000 to put together, was a good one and that the probability of a spill was extremely remote at best—one in 26 years. He defended the worst-case spill modeling in the plan and the assumptions it was based on. He said that almost any material that might be spilled would evaporate very quickly, three hours or less, and that the skimmer boats and booms Dow would keep on alert would prevent any chemicals from getting into the Suisun Marsh.

Bill Press wasn't satisfied. Why did Dow assume in its most recent calculations that a worst-case spill in the area of Suisun Marsh would be only 500,000 gallons when the tankers servicing the new complex would hold up to 5 million gallons? Perry could only answer that it was unlikely that all ten compartments in such a tanker would be broken open at the same time and, even so, any naptha would evaporate quickly. Press asked that Dow consider a more realistic case, to which Perry said he thought Dow could look into it.

Bill Ready of the California Waterfowl Association echoed Press' concerns about a spill and its impact on Suisun Marsh. He pointed out that there would undoubtedly be additional tanker traffic in the area if other plants followed Dow and if the Sacramento Channel was deepened as planned. He worried about the lack of control over shipping in the Straits of Carquinez.

According to Ready, ships in the straits were on their own in contrast to those plying San Francisco Bay, which has a sophisticated system to manage ship traffic. He said perhaps that explained why ships had occasionally rammed the Antioch Bridge (over the Straits of Carquinez just below the Suisun Marsh) and other area bridges during heavy fogs despite having the latest radar and electronics. In light of those incidents, Ready asked whether it was wise to rely on accident probability statistics for San Francisco Bay rather than the Straits of Carquinez. And what if, Ready asked, a Dow naptha ship hit an oil tanker? Had anyone considered that? Ready was also critical of what he claimed was the EIR's cursory treatment of the impact of increased salinity on Suisun, Grizzley, and Honker Bays.

During the remainder of the afternoon, Dow covered the economic and secondary growth impacts of the project. For the most part, the testimony was solid. It was clear that Dow would provide about 1,000 jobs directly and 2,700 overall. Tax revenues would be $12 million per year and consumers would benefit from lower product prices since Dow would save $56 million in transportation costs if it didn't have to ship products or raw materials from Texas or elsewhere.

Al Gunkler explained that the plant would be virtually self-sufficient with its own fire department, security guards, and water treatment facilities. The county wouldn't have to pay for any of this. Furthermore, most employees would be from the area so there wouldn't be that much residential growth and attendant demands for municipal and county services. And it was Dow's experience, claimed Gunkler, that the complex was unlikely to encourage a significant number of downstream plants.

The only flak that Gunkler ran into concerned the possibility of Dow buying land adjacent to its Pittsburg site from U.S. Steel rather than building across the river. One panel member said he had read that U.S. Steel no longer planned to expand its operations in Pittsburg and thus didn't need the land. Gunkler replied that Dow had tried to buy the land back in 1974, but it was too far down the road now with the Collinsville site to back off. "I think our interest in going through this again, starting over, is not too great." Gunkler also stressed the importance to Dow of having an undeveloped greenbelt around its new complex, but, under questioning, he would not commit Dow to leaving that land in open space in the future.

The evening session of the second day was the wildest and wooliest of all—Jack Jones' every fear come true.

Boy, it was a circus. There was a vice president from Dow. He was sitting in the audience and he watched all that going on. Dennis Banks— the Indian guy—got up there and the whole hearing panel stood up at reverent attention and Banks blabbered something in a sing-song sort of way and the hearing officer that night—who's now chairman of the Public Utilities Commission and former chief legal counsel for the Environmental Defense Fund and at that time was chairman of the Water Resources Board—he looked at him and said, "Would you favor us by translating those beautiful words into English?" And Dennis Banks said, "Oh well, sure—the water is blue and clean, and the sky is pretty and may the buffalo forever roam"—or some real innocuous thing like that. You'd of thought these guys were having an orgasm up there.

Well this guy from the home office looked at me and his eyes turned glassy and he said, "Unbelievable!" He gets up and walks out of the room, and I thought what the ——, it's blown here, so I ran out to calm him down. He said, "Jack, let's withdraw from the proceedings right now." I said, "We can't. We gotta go through with this. At least the governor hasn't reneged on his promise of a decision up or down within 30 days yet."

Jones' memory was a little faulty. Actually, it wasn't Banks who did the chanting but a medicine man named Moose Camp whom Banks had brought with him. Banks sang a song. But anyone who reads the transcript of the hearing that evening would have to concede it was a very cosmographic evening. Jerry Gilbert, whom Dow had decided not to put on the witness stand because of questions environmentalists had raised about his independence, sums it up in two words: "A disaster."

Bill Press later told me:

It was every bit as zany and dramatic as you imagine. My first premonition of trouble came when I heard the sound of tom-toms coming from the corridor outside the hearing room! Knowing what must have been going through the minds of Dow executives, I had a hard time keeping a straight face through the presentation. I was astonished to look around me when the song was finished and see several panel members with tears streaming down their faces! How do you explain that in Midland [Michigan, Dow's headquarters]?

Dennis Banks wasn't the only sideshow. Don Girod, speaking on behalf of the Ecobalance Planning Committee, a little-known environmental organization, babbled on for 15 minutes. His opening paragraph set the tone: "I think that, first of all, we have to learn that we are in a solar energy situation. We have the sun there as a constant source of solar energy, and it shines on our earth here and gives us a certain amount of life and a certain amount of biomass on the earth. So we don't have a dead planet." Girod went on to explore his version of the "pristine model" and the dangers of "ecocollapse." He declared his friendship with the mockingbirds and blackbirds. Sid McCausland of the California Lands Commission who was chairing the session, finally had enough and threatened to have Girod forcibly removed from the podium if he didn't wind things up.

Norman Repanich, speaking on behalf of the Solano County Industrial Development Agency, made a determined effort to even things out with a heart-wrenching, emotional plea to approve the plant: "We have heard the Fantus report; we have heard a whole lot of things. We can still encourage industry to locate in California, but, damn it, we are embarrassed when we get down to the bottom line and say 'Yeah, you can come.' We in Solano County are saying it. I have got seven resolutions here all supporting it. Someone is going to have to make the decisions somewhere along the line. You are going to have to say: Industry, yes or no. Just tell us."

Things actually did return to focus later in the evening. Marvin Sternberg of Friends of the Earth pointed out that allowing Dow to build might prevent smaller industries from siting in the area because air quality would be even worse. Robert Nevin, appearing on his own behalf, made a similar point—that air resources should be reserved for a greater number of cleaner industries. He was given prolonged applause by the audience. Nevin also pointed out that trees in California's mountains were dying from air pollution and warned that society was like an old-time miner whose "canary has died."

The panel also heard from a couple of local Collinsville farmers. One, Martin Sengo, criticized Dow's EIR for failing to do a detailed analysis of potential crop damage from the project's air pollution. McCausland, while recognizing the importance of Sengo's concerns, wondered if anyone could get all the answers: " . . . it suggested that perhaps the entire process of preparing an EIR is in need of review because we are essentially asking for information which is almost beyond human capability to provide. It's clear that the cost of providing it in each and every EIR would rapidly become prohibitive. Yet the questions are valid and I hope in these deliberations we can work towards some methodology that will help address those kinds of issues in a rational fashion."

Richard Brann, Solano County supervisor, brought the evening to a close. He argued that the Collinsville site, with its deep-water access, was a national resource for use by water-oriented industry. Brann also unveiled another justification for cancelling the Williamson Act contract that had been confidential until now: Mr. McOmie had placed some of the proceeds from the sale of his property in a trust that would be divided between the University of California at Davis and California Polytechnic State University for agriculture-related research. That, Brann maintained, would be a tremendous benefit to agriculture that would return more revenue than crops from the land could for many years.

When Brann finished, the hearings were adjourned until December 17, giving Dow an opportunity to work on the many questions raised about air pollution from the plant—questions that never seemed to end. Even the state officials were sympathetic. Sid McCausland opened the December 17 meeting with this lament: "I was recalling after the last session the many myths that I have read about ancient labyrinths or mazes and how before you get to the other world, you have to learn how to traverse the maze. And I think if we have ever had an opportunity in modern-day society to recreate the myth, we have done it. And we are here . . . in an analysis of whether or not there really is a way to get through the maze." McCausland ended, however, on a note of optimism: "I would like to suggest that there is a light at the end of the maze."

The first part of the morning session on the 17th was taken up by detailed testimony on Dow's air monitoring program. Dow had undertaken this expensive program for two very good reasons. First, it didn't trust BAAPCD's air quality data, which were based largely on monitoring done at Pittsburg and Fairfield, not at the Montezuma Hills site. Second, Dow wanted hard facts on air quality and meteorological conditions in the area—surely more reliable and probably more favorable than the "hocus pocus" modeling that Dow claimed BAAPCD relied on.

After reviewing its monitoring program, Dow spent the rest of the morning claiming that the proposed complex would have no effect on agricultural lands or crops in the Sacramento and San Joaquin Valleys. It was a tough assignment. Bill Beamer stated flatly that all the sulfur dioxide, oxidant, nitrous oxide, and ethylene emissions wouldn't cause any problems. That started another squabble with Tom Austin of the Air Resources Board.

Austin reminded Beamer that the ARB didn't buy Dow's earlier assertion that there wouldn't be any transport of smog-producing oxidants into the fertile San Joaquin Valley. Beamer started backing off and finally admitted there would be "some incremental effect. That's why we believe for the plant expansion to be acceptable there would have to be some mitigation of increases in emissions because we feel they definitely will contribute to the San Joaquin oxidant problem."

Austin was also troubled by Dow's emission figures for ethylene, a gas that produces such strange and varied effects in plants and seeds as wilting, early ripening, leaf droppage, and breaking of seed dormancy. For these reasons, it is classified as a plant hormone. The original EIR had projected emissions of 1.8 tons per day. That is a substantial amount, but the EIR failed to discuss what impact such emissions might have. Tomatoes, a big crop in the area, are particularly susceptible to ethylene. But now Dow was claiming that ethylene emissions would be only 10-15 percent of the earlier estimate. Beamer offered to go over the data with Austin after the hearings, but Austin wasn't happy. He argued that Dow's calculations assumed a pristine environment when in fact studies showed that crops in the immediate area were already suffering damage from sulfur dioxide and that significant amounts of ethylene were already in the air. Beamer asked for copies of those studies since he couldn't remember seeing them before.

Austin then took off on a tirade against Dow, claiming that the company was intransigent about mitigating the impact of emissions from the plant. He said other firms such as SOHIO, which was building an oil terminal in Long Beach, were searching for trade-offs, but that Dow "had shown zero interest in doing that so far." Ray Brubaker countered Austin, by pointing to the trade-off negotiations company officials had had with the ARB, EPA, and even Governor Brown. Brubaker was adamant, however, saying that Dow would not clean up nitrous oxide emissions as an offset against hydrocarbons. "I do not intend to purchase Standard Oil Company— and shut it down in order to accommodate the oxides of nitrogen in an area which is already in attainment." Austin got the final word in that afternoon. He said that without more information about emissions from Dow's power source, similar facilities in Texas and Louisiana, and tankers that would unload raw materials, "it's going to be difficult for the ARB to advise the various agencies regarding the acceptance of the proposal from an air quality standpoint."

The hearing panel turned next to the impact of the project on fish and wildlife. Dow stressed that it would actually improve the habitat for wildlife on its property through irrigation and management. Nobody disputed that, but Water Board representative Ray Dunham was bothered by Dow's failure to analyze its raw data on oil and chemical spills to determine their actual effect on waterfowl, fish, and other aquatic organisms. Dow conceded it hadn't gone that far, but Bob Lassen of the Department of Fish and Game said that waterfowl hadn't experienced any problems with the type of spills that might be expected. Bill Press also pointed out that the California Commission on Fish and Game had already granted three permits and asked if that wasn't proof that it was satisfied. But under questioning, the Fish and Game officials admitted that they hadn't done any real analysis of possible spills. They had made their decision on past experience, claiming they lacked the staff to do a more sophisticated analysis.

As the hearing entered its last hours, Dow talked about its plans to get rid of any hazardous wastes that might be generated. Dow had been a national leader in this field, promoting recycling rather than the landfill disposal favored by most in the industry. In fact, in 1972, company president Carl Gerstacker asserted Dow "would not consider landfill for waste disposal unless it is safe and truly the most effective method."[22] Dow was generally committed to that policy at Collinsville. Most of the liquid toxic wastes would be placed in evaporation ponds and eventually recycled. It would use technology that would be forced on the rest of the industry by the EPA in the early 1980s. The rest—from 2,000 to 5,000 barrels per month—would go to two local landfills and the most toxic material to Nevada.

Dow had an easy time of it on the hazardous waste issue. The approach it was taking was well above usual industry practice, and like elsewhere in the nation, California had only recently got into the hazardous wastes disposal field to regulate private sites, so there were few knowledgeable people around to offer informed comments. Six years later the state and nation would be more attuned to hazardous waste problems.

Art Shelton presented Dow's summation. Like his performance throughout, it was argumentative and pugnacious. To hear Shelton tell it, the Dow project simply didn't have any problems that couldn't be taken care of and, if people only listened, the inevitable truth would descend on them. Shelton warned that Dow wasn't going to go through the EIR process another time—it wanted an answer by the end of January. He closed by citing Dow's exemplary reputation in environmental protection. The Dreyfuss Third Century Fund— dedicated to investing in socially aware firms—ranked Dow first in environmental protection. He also cited *Business and Society Review* which had this to say about Dow: ''Most socially aware of all the chemical companies, [Dow] has crusaded vigorously for environmental protection measures in its own facilities and in those of other companies.'' That, according to Shelton, was the public's best guarantee that this project would not cause any environmental problems.

Finally, a number of local farmers, laborers, and other citizens who had waited patiently through three days of hearings got their chance to speak. They didn't really say much that hadn't been said before. But one, Louise Anderson, with whom I would later spend an afternoon, was more eloquent, more sincere, than almost anyone else. She talked about the good life this supposedly marginal land had given her family and the value of the land simply as an open space.

There are such beautiful areas along the river between Rio Vista and Collinsville and along the Montezuma Slough. I feel deeply that this should never be lost unless there is no other place where any industry that could destroy it could be located. This is sentimental trash talk to many people, I know, but I feel that there is a great need for people to live with nature wherever possible and that it's almost as important to one's sanity as eating and sleeping. You wouldn't believe the number of people who stop by our house every day seeking a little piece of land or just an old house to rent. And we, of course, are deluged all the time by fishermen and hunters. They act like they would live in a tepee if they could just have a little corner somewhere.

I believe this is Solano County's greatest potential, at least this part of it. If we must have industry, as it appears we must, then please can't we be terribly careful where we put it? The people here, for the most part, have little experience of heavy industry. They believed everything they were told about how great it was. Only now they are beginning to say, "It has its good points, but . . . ."

It isn't right that individual corporations have to go through so much, but until more is known about such problems as pollution—and interest groups try to rush things through before people do figure things out—what other solution is there? Our special interest groups are at present screaming because our supervisor hired a planning group to draw up three alternative plans for our county, but I am deeply grateful. Even if I should not be totally satisfied with whatever final conclusions are drawn, at least I will know that we have not rushed into things that we will later regret.

We understand the tremendous pressures being exerted on you and worry about it. We resent it, but know it's the American way. We approve a great deal of the many things your administration is trying to accomplish. We appreciate the way you seem to care for our state and its future. We wish you much wisdom and satisfaction in the choices you make.

Chapter 9

DOW GIVES CALIFORNIA THE BUSINESS

"It shook windowsills from Sacramento to San Diego." That's how one political pundit described Dow's decision to shelve its project. Jerry Brown had been in New York City on January 18, 1977, stroking a room full of big business types, extolling the virtues of California's business climate. The next day he got word that Dow had given the project its last rites because, according to a company press release, "the permitting process for new facilities has proved to be so involved and expensive it is impractical to continue."

Brown and other state officials were stunned. "The trial is over and the plaintiff left the courtroom just as the judge was about to give the verdict," Brown said. "I have to wonder why they didn't wait for the verdict." Jack Jones grins a bit when he recalls the shock Dow's decision caused. "Brown simply never thought Dow would quit. Some of Brown's staff told me since then that Brown was well aware we had spent 10 million bucks up to that point, so it seemed incredible that we would walk away. But they didn't know that January 31 was our absolute deadline for a decision."

Bill Press claims Dow would have had its decision—probably a "go"—shortly.

When Dow pulled out we had given ourselves seven weeks—in fact, the governor had said this is an absolute deadline—for making a decision on Dow. There was no guarantee that it would be a positive decision, but [it would be] a final decision. Dow knew this, in fact, because I had told them that our decision point was seven weeks or so away. They knew we had met with the Corps of Engineers and had succeeded in getting the Corps to agree to doing a joint EIS. Our supplemental EIR and their EIS would be a joint statement. That was the first time that had ever been done. This wasn't easy. The Corps is not known for being that cooperative with state agencies. They not only were willing to do a joint project but to meet our timetable. We were pursuing that, had put some money up for that and it was well on its way. The Water

109

Resources Control Board was the lead agency. We had people assigned to it and Dow knew that. Then suddenly, without really any warning [Press says, snapping his fingers for emphasis] Dow was gone. From my conversations with the people in the agencies, I was convinced that every one of those agencies would have approved the plan save the Reclamation Board, which had already denied the plant. But I was further convinced that after the other agencies had acted, the Reclamation Board, which really had very little jurisdiction—just over the levees—would go back and reverse its decision.''

Jack Jones recounts a different version of the last days of Dow.

The governor had promised we'd have a decision, up or down, within 30 days after the hearings. We sadly misjudged the governor in that respect, of course. When January 9th came around, we were presented a final opinion by Tony Kline, who was the governor's legal counsel, that said he agreed with the attorney general that this material from the hearings would have to be treated as new environmental information and would have to go back to start all over again through the EIR process. But they would try to expedite it. We said, ''You gave us a commitment to make a permit decision yes or no.'' They said, ''We can't honor that commitment.'' Press never did make a statement in January that they would have a decision in 45 days. He made that claim later to the press and when we asked him to recall for our memory when he made the statement, he couldn't do it. He said he thought [it] was assumed if they expedited it they could get the thing certified in 45 days. That was never done, but even if they had we probably wouldn't have believed them. We were completely out of time and saw no light at the end of the tunnel as to when we might start.

Al Gunkler adds that there was intense intracompany pressure for funds. ''You must understand that we are in constant competition for capital with the other divisions of Dow. We make a good story as to why it should be built out here, and our Texas and Louisiana friends are making a good story as to why they can expand incrementally and do better there. And all of this is a major problem.'' Ray Brubaker echoes Jones and Gunkler. ''When we got through the state hearings, the questions that came back and the comments that were made was that they were going to proceed to write an EIR for the state. So we were right all the time. That was another 90 days or so before they would begin to consider something else and on top of that we got another 100 questions back. It was about that time we decided we were not going to make progress and decided to quit, which we did.''

Given this bleak outlook, Brubaker says he recommended to top management in Midland that the project be dropped.

> The top people of Dow meet every year, usually in January, and they normally talk about people. But they also talk about a rolling capital program—when we spend a billion or two a year you've got to know what and where you're going to spend it over the next three years. They had been saving about a $150 million slot in the program for the Western Division. It came time to look at that. I recommended to management that they take that California project out, that it should not be holding up money that would otherwise be spent somewhere else in the world. They accepted that recommendation. We did not go away because of the problems with BAAPCD. Our real problem was with the statewide permits. We weren't making timely progress. With no positive results to show after spending two and a half years and $4.5 million to get four permits out of 65, I had to cut my losses.

Bill Press claims he was aware of the internal corporate struggle that was going on within Dow over capital funds, but thinks a crucial problem was what he says is the Western Division's second-class status within the company.

> That was one very real element. People in Dow and working with Dow told us the struggle was going on. The fact is that the United States Division is kind of a stepchild of the World Division now. And the Western Division has never had a major plant, a major investment. Basically they were on an option. The Board of Directors was really very demanding of them and skeptical of the ability of the Western Division to pull it off. I really think they had the rug pulled out from under them. I know that that decision was made at a board meeting that wasn't held in California. Ray Brubaker wasn't even there nor was Jack Jones. They received the word.

When environmentalists received the word, their first reaction was one of delight. A lobbyist for Bill Press' old organization, the Planning and Conservation League, gloated that "it was a victory for environmentalists in the sense that Dow wasn't able to snow the state . . . .It was a setback for business interests that don't want to meet the standards in the state of California." But that initial euphoria was swept away in a venomous outpouring of rage by business, labor, and chambers of commerce. The rush to blame was on and all fingers were pointed towards someone else—usually environmentalists.

Local officials were frothing at the mouth. "Solano County needs industry and I don't think we're going to get any cleaner industry. It probably means the end of industry trying to settle in Solano

County," claimed Carl Crawford, Suisun City planning director. Richard Brann accused the Brown Administration of giving only "lip service" to efforts to improve the permit process.

East Bay Area labor, industry, and political leaders called a meeting to protest the loss of the plant. Doyle Williams, labor official and leader of the labor-industry coalition COLAB, was cheered by 200 people as he visited the blame on Governor Brown. He threatened a one-day strike to make Brown "aware of what he and his administration are doing to the economy of California." State politicians chimed in. Assemblyman Dan Boatwright said he was "stunned" by the announcement. "We cannot blame Dow or any other company for pulling out of California. Red tape and bureaucracy are killing business." "I hope and pray it's not dead," Democratic Assemblyman John Knox added. "Every time we have a problem in California, we create a new government unit to issue a permit."

Republicans could hardly conceal their glee. Assembly Republican Leader Paul Priolo said the reason for the pullout was clear: "Brown's stringent regulatory policies, which are causing business and industry to avoid location here." San Diego Mayor Pete Wilson, who sported an impressive conservation record of his own, joined in the attack. He criticized Brown for not making more of an effort to get the Dow plant built. "This decision will probably cost California thousands of jobs once Dow's decision becomes common knowledge around this country and other business and industries are further discouraged form relocating to our state." Even some politically ambitious Democrats such as Lt. Governor Mervyn Dymally couldn't pass up the opportunity to skewer Brown. "The Dow experience will continue to haunt us," claimed Dymally. "The budget [of the Economic Development Department, which was supposed to help attract new industry] is embarrassing."

It didn't take long for the word to get around. The national press quickly picked up the story. *The New York Times*, the *Wall Street Journal*, and every major national business publication covered the Dow affair. Even the *Economist* carried a story. Corporate suites throughout the country were buzzing—what's wrong out there in California.

Pressure became so intense that EPA's regional office issued an unusual press release pleading that it had nothing to do with killing the Dow project. State environmentalists started to retreat, claiming they hadn't really wanted to torpedo the Dow project, but only to buy some more time for planning. The opposition wasn't buying that line, however, and the retreat started looking more like a rout.

The Chemical Manufacturers' Association took the unprecedented step of joining up with the building trades unions, the steelworkers, the Teamsters, and the United Auto Workers (UAW) to propose a legislative package designed to encourage investment and create jobs. A key element was the relaxation of air and water quality standards, and new rules for environmental impact analysis.

Influential State Sen. John Holmdahl wasted no time in convening a hearing "to find out just why Dow decided to pull out and if there is any possibility of a reconsideration." Larry King, who had written the letter from the attorney general's office that had broken Dow's back, says those hearings were a witch hunt. King was called on the carpet to explain his actions.

Clem Shute and I were called to the legislature when they had the hearings after Dow left. Dow got up and made a very gentlemanly-type statement. "We're not here to throw rocks at anybody, we're not here to cast blame." They really didn't kick anybody or make any squawks. But the legislator who was beating his own drum had no qualms. There were like three or four of them up there, conservative types who all had been fed certain things, obviously from the county supervisors or from Dow. Clem Shute and I finally get up to the podium after waiting half the day while these other people got up to be ridiculed. There was some little guy who came from BAAPCD who didn't even know what was going on. They just ran this poor old guy into the ground.

It was one of those things where if I hadn't been in the position I was in it would have been fun to do the McCarthy thing and try and turn it around on those who were asking the questions. But I had studiously avoided joining any environmental groups. I had no connections—Nick Yost, he's heading my unit, belonged to everything—but I'm up there with Clem Shute who had the same philosophy I did. And we were asked from a guy down south, "Mr. King, are you a member of the Sierra Club?" "No." "Mr. Shute, are you a member of the Sierra Club?" "No." Mr. King, are you now or have you ever been a member of any environmental group?" "No."

King cracks up with laughter. "The guy had to pass the baton because he was obviously going to find out that it was these insidious environmental types in there who were harassing poor Dow. We kind of perverted that among insiders to 'Are you now or have you ever been a member of any subversive organization like the Sierra Club or any other environmental group.' It was a witch hunt by those legislators."

King couldn't explain why Dow was such a model of decorum. Ray Brubaker, who had to take a lot of heat within the company, didn't say a cross word about Governor Brown, Bill Press, or any state agency. He offered constructive comments. He advised California to work on a trade-off system for air pollution, establish a clear concise program for granting or denying permits, and not to reduce environmental standards, just be more realistic in implementing them. Brubaker even complimented Governor Brown on his efforts to streamline the permitting process.

Bill Press was no different. He proposed that government regulators be given no more than one year to approve or reject a new industrial project. If an observer hadn't known better, he might have sworn the project had been approved. Why the sweetness? Quite simple. As Bill Press told me, "I made a deal with Brubaker that we wouldn't kick each other before the state legislature. Brubaker kept his side of that deal."

State senators and assemblymen quickly filled the legislative hopper with a bevy of bills designed to make sure that another siting fiasco didn't occur. One by Sen. John Nejedly from Contra Costa County gave agencies only 90 days to review project applications and make a final decision. Another proposal by a Republican from Orange County would have required anyone challenging approval of a project under CEQA, as the Sierra Club had done in this case, to post a bond equal to 5 percent of the project costs for any project more than $500,000—justice by toll gate, critics claimed. The Sierra Club would have been forced to come up with a bond of $25 million in its suit against Dow if that legislation had been on the books.

The Bay Area Air Pollution Control District also came under attack. Legislation was introduced to cut its independence by placing it under direct control of the Air Resources Board, which would have the power to weaken stricter local regulation.

Most of these bills, for one reason or another, didn't go anywhere, with one major exception. Democratic Assembly Speaker Leo McCarthy, another legislator with a good environmental record, didn't want to relax environmental standards, but was adamant that the process be speeded up. "I think developers deserve an early and prompt answer—up or down." He turned to Tom Willoughby, the respected chief of staff for the Assembly's Resources, Land Use, and Energy Committee, for help. Willoughby's answer was Assembly Bill (AB) 884.

"Up to that point," says Willoughby, "the legislature had been a spectator because the administration said they would get an answer by a certain date. Then Dow pulled out prior to that date and sort of blasted the state agencies for delays in issuing permits. In the realm of politics, the Republicans seized on that to talk about how the Brown Administration was ruining the business climate. It made the leaders in the legislature aware that there might be some short-comings in the way permits were processed and handled. They decided to take a look at the statutes to see if they could put together a way to expedite the permit process without weakening any environmental controls.''

Willoughby explained what AB 884 would do.

[The bill] was designed, one, to let the applicant know at an early stage what kind of information would be required by all of the various agencies that would grant permits. Secondly, to let the lead agency know what the scope of the environmental impact report was going to have to be for purposes of answering the needs of all the other agencies. And, thirdly, to give a fixed time period—18 months—for making a decision once a completed application was submitted. There were a lot of other little things added such as the fact that the agencies had to tell what other information was required if a company submitted an incomplete application. They had a set time to indicate what was deficient in the application. Once an application was submitted as completed then they couldn't keep going back and asking for more information, they couldn't keep having afterthoughts two or three months down the road and then say, hey, we just thought of some new questions we'd like to ask.

AB 884 sailed through the legislature and was on Governor Brown's desk for signature by September 1977. But Bill Press says Brown didn't like a number of features in it.

[He had] two problems with 884. Neither one originated in the governor's office. In the end it came down to signing a bill that had those two problems in it or not having a bill. In the end, I think the governor did the right thing. The first problem was that the jurisdiction of each agency was narrowed. The actual decision by the water board, for example, can only be made on water considerations. It couldn't consider growth impacts of a sewer. That is a part of AB 884 I strongly opposed. The first draft of the legislation came from the governor's office and then the speaker's staff worked very closely with us developing the bill. That particular provision came from them. Tom Quinn, John Bryson, and I very strongly opposed it. It came from Tom Willoughby. I still feel it's a step backward in terms of the comprehensive responsibility of some of the agencies. You cannot separate them.

The second problem with the bill is the one that says as long as there is outstanding litigation against a project the decision is not final. That can tie a project up forever. That's totally unacceptable and ought to be struck. You always have the option of going after a [temporary restraining order], and then it's up to the applicant if he wants to move

ahead. But certainly the state agency is not prevented from doing its
job. That came from Tom Willoughby. He felt very strongly about the
adequacy of EIRs. He offered that provision as an alternative when no
one would accept his first position to have a sort of court to rule on the
adequacy of EIRs that would give it a stamp of approval. I just saw
that as a whole new bureaucracy, just horrendous.

So AB 884 was not without its faults, but it does have a number of
strengths. Its strength is that it gets the state and local agencies together,
it sets deadlines where there weren't any before, it assigns definite
responsibility to OPR to make sure deadlines are met, and it requires
agencies to say up front what they'll require in a permit.

Perhaps showing that reforming the permit process can be as
difficult as navigating it at times, I was later told by one of OPR's
staff members that the provision about stopping the project until the
adequacy of an EIR was adjudicated actually originated in Press's
own office, a fact he was apparently unaware of.

Larry King's assessment of AB 884 is even more critical than
Press's. "It went after a lot of the perceived problems but didn't
touch on things like the sweetheart EIR that caused Dow problems.
The agencies can wriggle out of the deadline bind if they want to,
but it can be a trap for them. Is failure to act an approval without
any conditions or restrictions? And a waiver can always be extorted
from the applicant. Tom Willoughby is a very, very capable person
[but] not a lawyer. He does not understand a lot of the technical
side of things. You could write it, but don't you understand what
that's going to do to people? Commitments were made and it was
political. There were things he wanted to do for his boss. He is
capable, he's done a lot of good work over the years." So, King
says with a twinkle in his eyes, "I forgive him."

Despite these shortcomings Brown signed AB 884 into law to
take effect on January 1, 1978. Of course, anyone who follows
Jerry Brown knows that he wouldn't sit still when the waters around
him were churning. Brown would do something with a lot of fanfare
and symbolism. One of the first things he did was to turn around
his "era of limits" rhetoric, which had won the hearts of environmentalists. "Limits apply not only to business and government,
they apply to environmental groups as well," Brown said. "Up till
then," according to one wag, "Brown had been quoting Schu-
macher. Dow was really the focal point of the business climate
debate in California, which was huge. There was press coverage
every day for a long time. Brown knew he was in trouble. He
changed his rhetoric and attitude, and started hanging around with

folks like Milton Friedman.''

Brown's campaign was masterful. He took off on a well-publicized trip to Japan, at his own expense, to persuade Japanese automakers to build a plant in California. He started handing out buttons that said "California Means Business," he opened a new Office of Business and Economic Development charged with helping industry find sites and solving regulatory problems, and he appointed a respected San Diego banker to head the powerful Business and Transportation Agency. Columnists Robert Evans and Rowland Novak were moved. ''The darling of no-growth environmentalists . . . is bragging about California's recent economic growth and expressing hope for more—a sign of evolution of this most fascinating politician.''

''Window dressing,'' scoffs Michael Peevey, head of the business-oriented California Council for Environment and Economic Balance. ''The 'California Means Business' buttons were made in New Jersey because apparently they couldn't get them done quickly enough in California.'' The labor-business coalition that had supported Dow had fun with the buttons, producing their own with slogans like "Jerry Meditates While Dow Burns; Down with Brown, Up with Expectations; and California Means Business—We're No. 47.''

But, in truth, Brown did make some important substantive moves and his attitude toward business did change. Bill Press agrees.

> There was definitely a swing after Dow toward the right. [It was] an open attempt to seek a rapprochement with business because Dow confirmed all the worst statements about California having a bad business climate and not being a place for a major investment. The attitude in the administration at that time wasn't anti-business. People weren't aware of some of the things we were doing for business, so what we tried to do at that time was to do a little better public relations with some of the things that were going plus bringing people in like Dick Silberman [formerly a successful banker and fast-food marketer] who did a tremendous job of building bridges with the business community. I don't think, however, that went too far. Brown started to balance his public statements and that's about where things stand today.

Brown's people also worked hard to enact legislation that would streamline the permitting process (AB 884) and on a proposal to map out sites suitable for industry throughout the state and in the Bay Area. Brown also threw his weight behind efforts to repeal or modify several taxes, such as an inventory tax, that businesses found particularly grating. In another move that rankled environmentalists, Brown came out strongly in support of building a liquefied natural gas (LNG) complex on an undeveloped stretch of California's coastline, eventually supporting a bill designed specifically to get that complex built quickly by putting the more development-oriented Public Utilities Commission in charge of siting.

Perhaps even more important are the changes the Dow affair wrought in the way state agencies dealt with big projects. California agency officials realized that unnecessary delay wasn't going to be tolerated. If they wanted to stay out of the frying pan, they had to act in a timely fashion. That's not to say they had to approve a project, only that they had to say yes or no as quickly as possible. This is of crucial importance to business, not so much because of the potential savings in money, but because most corporations plan new facilities to meet a projected demand at a specific time, in effect, a market window. That window is typically small and any inordinate delay may slam it shut. Jerry Gilbert, Dow's EIR consultant who has now turned his attention to water conservation projects, says that the process is more streamlined now so that there is "accepted delay." "Planners know now how long it will take and just factor in into their plans. Whether the delay is justified or not is another question." Gilbert also feels that the regulatory climate has changed. "The boards now take a more balanced approach and don't act so arbitrarily. There used to be a populist citizen-oriented feeling in state agencies and not much interest in the technical or scientific perspective. We're beginning to see a change there too."

All of this led John Zierold, a long-time staff lobbyist for the Sierra Club, to warn that "California politics has not yet seen the last of the Dow affair. Ill winds continue to blow and elected weathercocks to spin . . . the conservationist is back between the shafts of the ragman's cart." Zierold and other environmentalists were quick to realize that a horrific backlash had begun. Cynthia Kay, who had spearheaded the opposition to Dow, recalls the pressure. "Nick Arguimbau and I were running scared. We never believed we'd stop the whole development, and now we thought we might end up losing CEQA. Bill Press called a meeting at his house with environmentalists. He said that there was terrific pressure from industry to react. John Zierold said we were in trouble. Out of that meeting emerged AB 884."

Kay says that the "victory" against Dow also led to infighting among environmentalists. "There was a hasty debate within the task force on how to pull our horns back. Some wanted to put the Dow plant some place, but they couldn't decide where. Some were elitist and said let the dumb suckers in Pittsburg get it. They are elitist and I didn't want to be associated with that so I dropped out."

Michael Storper claims environmentalists had other reasons for being scared. He says that Jack Jones unleashed a "systematic campaign against all of us in the opposition."

For example, Ellen Widess, then a professor at U.C., had consulted with Friends of the Earth on land use questions. Jones wrote to her department chairman, and to the press, accusing her of basing grades in her classes on student participation and advocacy in the Dow case. Similarly, he accused us of not really representing Friends of the Earth, and others of not really representing the Sierra Club.

Just last year, Dow proposed a similar petrochemical complex in Alaska, and the local public television station up there did an hour-long documentary on it. They sent a film crew down to the Bay Area to interview Ellen, who is now an attorney for the state Occupational Safety and Health Administration. After the program was aired, not only did Jack Jones personally demand rebuttal by the TV station, but he wrote to the head of Ellen's agency and accused her of using state time and state endorsements for fighting Dow, which were patently false.

Apparently environmentalists didn't just pull their horns back, but underwent a sex change—from roosters to chickens. John Zierold wrote in 1978 that "Tom Quinn, the Governor's smog sentinel, called a meeting in Los Angeles with environmental leaders, to whom he delivered a message that Jerry Brown thought the environmental movement was dead because the heat was coming only from industry, and that Brown might shortcut the permit process because no one was insisting that he shouldn't."[23]

But Brown didn't abandon his environmental constituency, Bill Press maintains. "If anything, the pendulum in terms of public policy emanating from the administration has swung back the other way. The environmentalists may have lost at Dow, but they won a major victory at Sundesert [a nuclear power plant] and Diablo Canyon, which are, in the end, much more significant decisions than Dow Chemical in my opinion. Dow is so huge in symbolism and yet, when you come down to it, it is so small in terms of investment, jobs, or impact on the California landscape."

One of Brown's biographers recounts how adroit the governor had been: "Then, just as Brown has thoroughly incited environmentalists by his dalliance with business, he will announce that the Grumman Corporation . . . has been convinced to build a million-dollar solar-heating-unit factory in the San Joaquin Valley. Coming as it does on top of a Brown-backed bill to give homeowners a tax credit of 55 percent—up to a maximum of $3,000—for the purchase and installation of these heaters, such announcements throw both sides of the enviro-business struggle into disarray."[24]

After a year of Brown's wooing, some state businessmen began to respond. "If you had asked me six months ago [about the Brown Administration's attitudes toward economic development], I would have given you a different answer," said Robert Draine, executive vice president of Coldwell Banker and Co., a large industrial real estate brokerage concern, in a *Wall Street Journal* interview. "Now I think they're getting the message."[25] However, most executives in the chemical industry weren't convinced. In March 1978, the Manufacturing Chemists Association held a seminar in California focusing on the theme: "Should the chemical industry write California off?" Many of the participants agreed with DuPont Senior Vice President Richard Herbert. "We probably will not build in California or any other state with a permit process that's as cumbersome." In an article about the meeting, *Chemical Week* reported that within companies, western managers "are said to find themselves often in a losing battle to convince their own eastern board members and senior executives of the wisdom of investing in the Golden State."

Alan Stein, Brown's secretary of business and transportation, defended California's tough environmental controls and claimed that the Dow proposal could win state approval if it was resubmitted. That drew a sharp attack from Paul Oreffice, then-president of Dow Chemical U.S.A.: "You are assuming the chemical industry is coming here to destroy the environment. No industry in the world has spent more money than the chemical industry of the United States to clean up the environment. I submit to you there is a problem with attitude in state government in California. We have other states in this country that live with the same Environmental Protection Agency rules but have an entirely different attitude."

Up to that point, however, Dow had maintained a fairly low profile, offering little public criticism of California. In 1978, Ray Brubaker did publish a short article in *Industrial Development*, a rabidly anti-environmentalist trade magazine. In that piece, entitled "A Rocky Road Awaits Industry on Its Way through the Environmental Obstacle Course," Brubaker presented a somewhat one-sided picture of the Dow "episode," although the tone of the piece was less hostile and hysterical than in other articles sometimes found in that magazine. But the company generally stayed quiet. One Dow official from Midland told me: "I think our people realize that top management wasn't attuned to new planning realities in the Solano

County dispute. They were operating in the past." Nevertheless, Jack Jones claims that the debacle did not lead to any changes in the way Dow planned for big projects. Ray Brubaker agreed: "I'm not aware of any changes. We live in relative peace with the environmental people wherever we are."

But apparently the California experience had seriously angered top Dow executives. In an interview several months later, Oreffice, who by now had climbed to the presidency of Dow, again vented his spleen. When asked what he learned from that case, he responded: "The lesson is an old one. It is that the environmental movement has to be brought to its logical boundaries. And I think the tax revolution will make it happen. We are victims of environmental overkill and I believe the survival of this country as a free society is at stake."[26]

This was certainly a different tune than Dow had sung only a few years earlier and it would set the tone for a virulent anti-regulatory campaign Dow would embark on. Dow's 1978 annual report led off with a piece entitled "Federal Over-Regulation: Draining Human Resources and Feeding Inflation." It alleged, among other things, that Dow's Pittsburg plant required 563 separate air permit applications each year. It also complained about the air pollution problems the company was having in Midland. A relatively poor showing by Dow U.S.A. was attributed, in part, to "unrelenting growth of government regulatory activity [that] . . . required a continuing diversion of resources into non-productive applications."

The blitz continued over the next two years. Oreffice frequently quoted a study he had commissioned that concluded federal regulations were the company's fastest growing cost—$186 million in 1976 alone for Dow U.S.A. Dow also fought EPA over regulation of toxic chemicals and pesticides such as 2,4,5-T. David Rooke, President of Dow U.S.A., proclaimed that "Dow believes in fighting. We hung in on napalm when it didn't mean anything to us businesswise."

In a remarkable turnabout, Dow had become known as the most militant of the chemical companies. By 1980, the company was included in a "Dirty Dozen" list of corporations by a group of militant environmentalists, in part because Dow was contributing substantial sums to politicians with poor environmental records.

The Dow affair sent its shock waves to the nation's capital. EPA, under great pressure to allow growth in areas with dirty air, pushed for revisions in the Clean Air Act to allow a company locating in a nonattainment area to buy up "offsets" from existing firms so that the new plant could be built—something the BAAPCD wouldn't let Dow do back in 1976. There was also a great uproar over the question whether some states, such as Texas and Louisiana, were playing games with federal environmental standards in an effort to attract new industry. Rumors abounded that the governors of Texas and other southern states telephoned Dow immediately after it pulled out of California inviting the company to locate its facility in their jursidictions, with promises that environmental poblems would be taken care of. Another chapter in the continuing Frostbelt-Sunbelt fight was being written.

In California, a favorite pastime was guessing where the Dow plant really went. Almost every person I talked with had his own theory, whispered to me in hushed tones after a quick glance around the room to see if someone might be eavesdropping. "Don't tell anyone I said so, but I have it from inside Dow that the plant went to Korea." "No, it was split between Texas and Louisiana." "Most definitely went to British Columbia." The problem is, with a big multinational such as Dow, it is virtually imposible to determine where the capacity really went. British Columbia, where Dow has recently built a new plant, probably makes more sense simply because it is closest to the California market.

The Environmental Protection Agency responded to the rumors about siting by organizing a special task force to investigate the charges that some states were being "flexible" with environmental laws in their chase for smokestacks. At the head of that task force was Paul DeFalco, who had been involved in the Dow affair as head of EPA's regional office in San Francisco. DeFalco was unable to find any concrete evidence to substantiate those claims.

Politicans, businessmen, and environmentalists also debated whether tough domestic environment controls were driving industry abroad. A 1978 study alleged that the United States was on the verge of a "wholesale exodus" of major pollution-intensive industries. The report by Barry Castleman, a Washington-based chemical engineer, claimed " . . . the economy of hazard export is emerging as a driving force in new plant investment in many hazardous and polluting industries."[27] The issue became so sensitive that at the Geneva Trade Talks in 1979 Robert Strauss, who was the U.S. special representative for trade negotiations, raised this very issue: "American standards in these areas are among the highest in the world, and we do not want this U.S. willingness to protect the environment and our workers to disadvantage the various U.S. producers will to pay such costs."[28]

By 1980, things had settled down in California. Perhaps it is revealing that while U.S. business magazines were running articles in 1977 about California with titles like "Paradise Lost," the English *Economist* looked at the state's prospects and predicted, correctly, that California would bounce back quickly. Contrary to the doomsayers of 1977, today the state's economy is stronger than ever, with an unemployment rate less than the national average. One crystal-ball economist from the Bank of America summarized the state's prospects: "I think we'll do in a range of moderately to a hell of a lot better than the rest of the country."

Of course industries aren't rushing to California just for the pleasure of being tortured by the state's still strong environmental laws, but to a large extent, California's natural advantages—climate, huge market, trained work force, and natural resources—simply outweigh any impediments. The reforms enacted in 1977 together with an increased sensitivity among state agencies about industries' problems in the permitting process, have improved things to a certain extent. And, to industry's delight, a new Republican attorney general, George Deukmejian (who would later run for governor against Tom Bradley of Los Angeles), dismantled the proud environmental unit, scattering people like Clem Shute and Larry King. True, California did give us the celebrated SOHIO Pactex oil terminal case at Long Beach, which almost led to the establishment of a national energy mobilization board, but aside from that much-publicized debate, business has been building a lot of offices, warehouses, and plants in California. Overall, the state gained more manufacturing employment during the 1970s than any other state in the Union. Most observers agree, however, that in the overall scheme of things, the Proposition 13 tax cut, a tremendous boon for business, has done more to improve California's business climate than any tinkering with environmental laws could ever accomplish.

Some business leaders in California have gone so far as to say that the Bay Area is probably better off without Dow. The number of jobs it promised were relatively few and the additional air pollution might have precluded development of cleaner, more labor-intensive businesses. Contemplating the tremendous growth the San Francisco region has experienced in the past few years, Angelo Siracusa, head of the Bay Area Council, a moderate business-oriented group, asked "whether we might not be able to make our living out here taking in other people's laundry, providing services rather than working in big factories?" Whether or not the San Francisco region can survive without heavy industry is debatable, but it is clear that the area's growth has been linked more closely to light industries such as computers—the "Silicon Valley" is in the southern part of the Bay Area—that pollute less.

And what about Dow's Solano County site? Physically, the area hasn't changed a whit. The wind still blows hard across the Montezuma Hills. Stan Anderson still farms as he did in 1975. The air hasn't got much better. And Solano County continues to grow rapidly as people push out of the Bay Area in search of affordable housing.

But the industrial future of the area is still up for grabs. The major legal roadblocks Dow faced have, to a great extent, been removed or eased. What had appeared to be insurmountable air pollution problems were taken care of very quickly. While the BAAPCD had appeared to some to be intransigent toward any changes in its new plant review regulations, which had stymied Dow, perhaps Ray Brubaker was right when he told me he always thought that eventually Dow would get air pollution permits. In December 1977, just 11 months after Dow pulled out, the BAAPCD responded to pressure from the state Air Resources Board and the EPA and adopted new regulations. These regulations were very much along the lines that Dow had wanted and that were already in use in other states.[29] As a result, Paul DeFalco told me, "There's no doubt in my mind that Dow could get approval of air pollution permits to build that plant today."

And neither did Solano County waste any time going back to patch up its comprehensive land-use and development plan for the area. It produced a credible document that leaves no doubt industrial development can proceed around Collinsville.

The Williamson Act contract, intended to preserve the land for agricultural use, could still be a problem. In late 1980, the California Supreme Court ruled that such contracts could be cancelled only in "extraordinary" or "unforeseen" circumstances. So, Larry Silver of the Sierra Club was right all along—the county's cancellation was almost certainly invalid. In the wake of that decision, however, several bills were introduced in the state legislature to gut the Williamson Act. A compromise measure finally passed establishing a "window" from January to May of 1982 during which time farmers could cancel contracts. Dow missed that "window," but in any case the contract on its land will run out soon, allowing it to proceed with development by 1984 if it chooses to.

But most people don't expect an industrial development boom any time soon. The chemicals market is soft due to the current recession, and Dow has plenty of capacity elsewhere. The recession has also put a hold on (and perhaps killed) expansion plans of other big industries like ARCO and U.S. Steel. Pacific Gas and Electric gave up on its Collinsville site and won preliminary state approval for a huge coal-fired plant 10 miles inland. But even those plans have been shelved. People are using less electricity, and the state regulators are now less amenable to big construction plans. Many doubt whether a new plant will ever be built.

Even if the economy soon perks up, some people doubt whether Dow would have smooth sailing in spite of changes in environmental laws. There is heightened awareness among citizens in the area about the down side of industrial development. A state-financed project found 21 abandoned chemical dumps in Contra Costa County, many containing significant levels of DDT, lead, and asbestos.

In 1978, the state also began a cancer study in an attempt to find out why male workers in the area had such a high rate of lung cancer, 40 percent higher in industrial areas of the county than in nonindustrial sections. A preliminary report from the study concluded that the higher rate was linked to occupational exposure, not ambient air pollution. But when a *New York Times* reporter ventured into Contra Costa County, he found a good deal of skepticism.[30] "Sometimes the pollution has been so bad that it would peel the paint off our cars," claimed 65-year-old Mr. Edgar Monk, a long-time resident who suffers from asthma and blames air pollution for his poor health. "It has different smells. Sometimes it smells like rotten eggs or old cabbages. It burns the nose and throat." Five hundred other residents petitioned the county board of supervisors to pass a resolution demanding the right to know which chemicals and toxic substances are stored, used, and dumped in their neighborhoods.

Water quality and quantity in the Delta have been hot issues, too, with the debate focused on the now-defeated Peripheral Canal that would have sucked water from the area and sent much of it south to Los Angeles. While a certain animosity toward Los Angeles was probably a dominating factor in this defeat, in addition to the canal's enormous costs, people also worried about the possibility of severe environmental damage to the Delta, San Francisco Bay, and their fisheries. Thus, Dow would have to face a citizenry more concerned about issues like water supply and pollution than it did in the mid-1970s.

Chapter 10

THE LESSONS OF DOW[31]

The players in the Dow controversy were in many ways like a toddler taking its first steps. The baby careens around a room, runs into things, and finally falls down. But, the next time around the trip goes more smoothly.

Many people forget that Dow was like a guinea pig, testing a host of environmental laws, both state and national, that had only recently been enacted. In 1969, there were hardly any effective environmental laws on the books. Then came Earth Day in 1970; five years later, corporations had to deal with not only a host of new laws but a new mood in the country. A 1970 Gallup survey asked which three national problems the government should devote most attention to in the next year. An amazing 53 percent listed reducing air and water pollution, second only to reducing the amount of crime, which garnered 56 percent.

Dow was one of the first to test the Clean Air Act as it applied to building plants in areas with dirty air, one of the earlier major industrial developments to go through the California state environmental impact process, and one of the first to face the problem of protecting critical wetlands, whose value was only being realized after years of dredging, filling, and polluting marshes across the nation. In each instance the law was improved after Dow.

Indeed, the word got all the way back to Washington. EPA under President Carter showed far greater sensitivity to regulatory glitches than did other bureaucracies such as the Federal Trade Commission. It devised an offsets policy that would have helped Dow, although admittedly its implementation is proving extremely complex and difficult. And at the President's Council on Environmental Quality, Nick Yost, Larry King's old boss in California, spearheaded a major overhaul of environmental impact analysis required under NEPA. Yost candidly told me that he drew heavily on what he learned in California.

The message also went out to agencies in other states which have responded with an innovative and diverse array of mechanisms to make the permitting process more efficient, ensuring that a project is reviewed thoroughly but expeditiously. California has an Office of Permit Assistance, Colorado a promising special review process for major energy projects that stresses cooperation rather than confrontation, Florida a highly effective power plant siting act, and Georgia a truly consolidated one-stop shopping system for environmental permits. They are new and, while none works perfectly, each holds promise to grease the regulatory mechanisms in such a way that the machine keeps running while we search for even more effective means to reconcile economic development and environmental protection. Importantly, these measures do not require radical reorganizations, nor the establishment of a big federal board (like the Energy Mobilization Board) to ramrod things, or another big bureaucracy.

That's not to say these less ambitious reforms are easy to effect. Ask Bill Press. He tried to put together a state industrial siting plan that would tell people where to build, as opposed to where not, but the results were disappointing because local governments retained the power to implement the plan and few wanted the state telling them what to do. Similarly, a siting plan developed by the Association of Bay Area Governments, a regional planning organization, fell through because local governments fought over details like who would get preference for clean industry, who would take heavy industry, and so on.

And rearranging agencies or building bridges among various governments won't solve everything. Sometimes industry has problems with the permit system because regulators—who often work for a pittance and little prestige—are inexperienced or overworked. With state and local budgets tight, there is little prospect of relief if the federal government withdraws from the field.

Environmentalists have a role to play, and they have been busy since they sniffed the change in the wind that blew out of California. A new breed, called mediators, has emerged to help cool tempers and look for nonjudicial solutions in environmental battles. They operate from the principle that if both sides are willing to sit down and talk, it may be possible to slice the pie up in such a way that everyone is happy—or at least to prevent people from being mad enough to bring the house down.

The idea has been carried further by some public interest groups that have applied it at a policy level. Here, the idea is to get various interests—industry, government, environmentalists—together to consider a particular environmental problem—say, for example, hazardous wastes—and attempt to reach a consensus position that can be conveyed to policy makers. I have sat in on one such effort, and it is truly amazing to see the progress that can be made in a quiet, constructive atmosphere where people don't feel they have to make speeches or posture for the benefit of a particular constituency. There are potential shortcomings in these approaches. For example, the public at large can be excluded from having a real say in matters, as it often was prior to the 1970s. But these new approaches hold enough promise to warrant further exploration as a way to solving disputes more efficiently.

Along this same line, Congress has been considering a regulation-negotiation bill—"reg/neg" in the lingo of Capitol Hill—that bears watching. The theory behind reg/neg is that the existing process of establishing regulations is one that prompts each interested party to express its own self interest as forcefully and skillfully as possible. Opposing coalitions often develop, each accepting the role of advocate in an adversarial process. Communication with an opposing side is often viewed as a sign of weakness. Could we produce more effective, efficient regulations if the process emphasized consensus rather than confrontation? Bills before Congress would establish experimental regulatory negotiation commissions with a mandate to bring affected parties together to negotiate over proposed regulations or regulatory policy. Any consensus or points of disagreement would then be reported to relevant government agencies that, while not bound by the results, would have a far better idea of what regulations might be acceptable to and supported by a broad range of interests.

The Dow affair also has a great deal to say about the way corporations will need to plan for and build projects in the 1980s. While some industrialists view the backlash to Dow and similar fights as an opportunity to weaken environmental and land-use laws, opinion surveys indicate they will be sadly mistaken if they think the public's commitment to the environment is dead or even seriously compromised. Polls taken by ABC News/Harris, CBS News/New York Times, the National Opinion Research Center at the University of Chicago, and Resources for the Future all indicate continued strong support for environmental protection. As the Opinion Research Corporation advised in 1977, after conducting a poll on environmental issues:

> All told, if public opinion is any guide, it would seem that business continues to have little recourse but to learn to cope with the fact that environmental protection no longer is the exclusive domain of a handful of professional social critics and environmental activists, but the continuing concern of the public as a whole.

All of which is not surprising. The attitude of people in this country toward the environment has changed fundamentally in the last decade. Just as many social programs like Social Security were viewed as radical initiatives when first proposed, they are now a given in our lives. Everybody I talked to within the Dow controversy, Dow's people included, described themselves as either an environmentalist or a conservationist.

The old way of building plants simply will not pass muster in the 1980s. No longer can corporations consider environmental constraints as an afterthought. The day the idea for a facility is hatched, someone must ask whether the project will have an adverse impact on a special place—a marsh, a scenic river, a pristine coast—because it is the risk that such places will be despoiled that will likely generate opposition. If it will, then the question must be asked whether there are alternative sites available. If not, how can adverse impacts be mitigated? In short, corporations must seek out sites that have a fighting chance of success from an environmental point of view. They will also have to be particularly sensitive to secondary growth impacts of big projects.

And in selecting someone to guide a project through the permit system, corporations will do better with mediators than brawlers. Knowing the local boys and being a fighter won't be enough in the 1980s. Neither will being a law school classmate of the corporation's general counsel—the way some firms now select local project counsel. The new project advisor will be someone who knows the state agencies inside out and can deal with them in a low-key fashion. State agencies will have the say-so in the next decade, since practically all federal environmental programs will be delegated to the states by then. Already, a fraternity of state-oriented practitioners with impressive track records is springing up around the country. Some work inside corporations while others are in private practice, many are attorneys, but others are planners, engineers, and the like.

Perhaps one of the most interesting aspects of the Dow controversy is that Dow did not change the way it plans for projects. Maybe it did not need to. Beckee Beemer, who helped handle environmental permits for Dow before she left for another firm, says Dow could have done better in California, but that overall its philosophy on environmental problems is a good one—"clean out the skeletons before anyone finds them." But, if anything, the signals coming down from top executives like Paul Oreffice seem to indicate to project and plant managers that it's time to fight environmentalists. Perhaps that's why Jack Jones, who is now lobbying for Dow in Sacramento, felt secure in telling me about an old barn he had ordered knocked down on the McOmie Ranch. I had commented that the old weathered redwood barns sprinkled about the Montezuma Hills added to the atmosphere of the place. Jones bragged he had demolished one before those "pseudo-environmentalists" could get it listed as an historic landmark.

Until middle-level executives get the message that environmental considerations are important, they will continue to look at the short-term bottom line—and to most, practicing environmental conservation doesn't appear to add much to the equation. It will take more than corprorate leaders giving occasional speeches about how they are environmentalists. Fundamental changes in corporate organization will be necessary so that project planners and plant managers are not penalized for making the long-term environmentally preferable choices in a particular situation. Until they do, future disputes with regulators and environmentalists are inevitable.

Business schools could play a crucial role in this readjustment, but most have not yet begun to do so. Few offer any courses in the environmental aspects of project planning. In 1980, Stanford, for example, devoted only a few class periods in a general course on social responsibility to environmental aspects of project planning. I talked with some students there who never heard of the fight Dow had only a few miles to the north. Yet, spokesmen for big business constantly complain about the problems environmental regulations are causing in building new plants, which makes one wonder if the squawking isn't a lot of hyperbole or whether business schools are simply out of touch with what is happening in the real world.

Business schools respond that they aren't in the business of training environmental specialists, only in teaching students how to think. I remember hearing that argument at the University of Chicago Law School used to justify the relatively restricted curriculum offered to its students. There is something to be said for that position—it is more important for an aspiring environmental lawyer to learn the basics and to think like a lawyer than to become an instant expert in law school. But, still, almost every law school, including the University of Chicago, now offers an elementary environmental law course just as they offer courses in other regulatory areas such as anti-trust that are likely to be of great significance to future lawyers and their clients.

It seems the height of folly not to give our future business leaders a similar exposure from a management perspective, not as an elective in the law school or some other department.

While a majority of schools cling to traditional ways, there are a few encouraging signs. The New York University Graduate School of Business has work underway on alternative methods of dispute resolution and Stanford University's business school has recently begun offering courses on the impact of government regulation on corporate planning and decision making.

Corporations will also have to open their project planning process in a way that many will find difficult. If we have learned anything from the Dow case and a host of other environmental disputes, it is that companies must be prepared to let the public know what is going on at a very early stage in the game. By failing to meet the vinyl chloride issue early on and by failing to have a spill control plan in hand at the outset of the environmental impact process, Dow appeared either to be hiding something or callously disregarding a potential environmental threat. This lent ammunition to the opposition. Openness alone will not guarantee success, but it can act as an insurance policy for a favorable, timely decision.

A number of corporations have already faced up to this new reality. AMAX Corporation is currently engaged in what many consider to be the model for future major developments as it plans for a massive molybdenum mine in southern Colorado. Because the mine project was so big and promised to be highly controversial given the area's scenic beauty, AMAX agreed to become a guinea pig for something called the Colorado joint review process (CJRP). The CJRP is a voluntary mechanism designed to coordinate local, state, and federal permitting procedures so that decisions are made more expeditiously based on a full environmental analysis.

Most importantly, CJRP seeks to involve government agencies and the public early in a company's project planning so that all environmental issues are identified early on, thus helping to avoid conflict and litigation at later stages. Agencies set voluntary deadlines for issuing permits or making decisions, but no environmental laws are waived under CJRP. While the verdict is still out on this new approach, one AMAX official has stated: "We think this has more promise than anything we've seen."[32]

All these changes by federal and state agencies, corporations, and environmentalists will be helpful, but perhaps the most important lesson that Dow and other siting controversies teach us is that we are unlikely to accomplish reforms—be they in corporations, state agencies, or in citizen attitudes—overnight, nor in one fell swoop. Early reforms will have to be reformed, and to win reformers will have to gird for the long haul, undaunted by past failures like the Dow case, learning from them and not looking back to fix blame.

Perhaps Jerry Brown said it best: " . . . there are only incremental adjustments. To do anything more is naive . . . because mammoth, comprehensive reform plans almost always boomerang—in the unlikely event they are passed.'' The Dow case helped California and the nation focus on changes that were needed right away, but it raises a number of more subtle and, I believe, more important issues.

First, Dow highlights the problems inherent in evaluating the social, economic, and environmental impact of a big project and mitigating the adverse ones. Not many people are in favor of long unemployment lines, and, at the same time, few want to ruin a critical wetland. Yet, because this nation will need to create many jobs in the 1980s, decision makers will be forced to proceed with less than perfect information. There will be no way to completely avoid that problem, but it must be minimized to the greatest extent possible.

To a certain extent, the courts have dealt with one problem that plagued Dow—just how much speculating did the company have to do in writing its environmental impact statement. Should it have discussed what impact the plant's products would have in southern California? Should Dow have undertaken more original research to answer questions raised by the state agencies? A number of recent cases interpreting the National Environmental Policy Act answer those questions with a clear "no." Generally, remote and speculative consequences of a project need not be discussed, nor does NEPA require a proponent to initiate special studies; action may proceed on the best available information.[33]

But, merely narrowing the scope of NEPA will not solve the problem. What of states or local governments that adamantly oppose major projects of regional or national significance? Clearly, it will not be acceptable to let local governments have complete sway over such developments. On the other hand, the Energy Mobilization Board solution, which puts the federal government in the driver's seat, is not at all appealing to many. The trick will be to balance local, state, and national needs.

In some instances local governments may oppose a project vital to the country. Areas like Collinsville may indeed be national resources for one reason or another, perhaps because of deepwater access, perhaps because a vital mineral is located there, and thus the national interest may dictate development. But while the most highly publicized cases are those where a local government fought a project tooth and nail, in reality, most local jurisdictions in the United States still welcome growth. Put another way, California is California and the small towns on the eastern seaboard that fought oil refineries are in the minority.

Industry needs to play that card with caution, however. Even in the West, where growth often seems to be a synonym for apple pie, local governments and residents are beginning to demand more careful evaluation of project impacts. Gunnison County, Colorado, cowboy country where people can do with their property as they please, has learned from the sad experience of energy boom towns like Gillette, Wyoming. Gunnison is carefully planning for growth—the county will almost double in size if AMAX's big molybdenum mine and other planned industrial projects are built—in such a way as to preserve ranching, tourism, and wilderness too.

Thus, as pollster Louis Harris observed in 1978, the public is willing to take many risks, particularly because of the energy shortage, but it is also shaking a stern finger in the face of those responsible and saying: "But don't you dare relax your all-out efforts to make certain that environmental hazards are kept to an absolute minimum."[34]

It is in cases such as Gunnison County where industry must be on its best behavior. An exemplary performance in places where people still say okay to development will, I believe, reap rewards. But small jurisdictions will need help, and this is the other side of local government control. Solano County, with its small planning staff of 12 people, was roundly criticized for being too unsophisticated to cope with the big Dow project. Perhaps it was, but the fact is that Solano County is light years ahead of many jurisdictions across the country. Many rural areas in the United States have no zoning at all, let alone the financial resources, staff, or will to cope with growth! And demographic trends and major industry growth predictions indicate that it is precisely those places, with their inexperienced, somewhat ingenuous local government officials, where so much new growth will take place in the 1980s.

If industry follows the lead of progressive companies like AMAX and helps localities plan for big projects and avoid the serious environmental impacts, then it will regain much of the luster it lost during the environmental battles of the 1970s. If it does not, the pendulum will assuredly swing back toward ever stricter environmental and land-use controls as the strong environmental feelings of the early 1970s are rekindled.

This will mean more than just making sure that emissions from a big plant meet federal pollution standards. Industry will have to concern itself with the incremental aspects of growth that comes with its projects—the effect of a population influx on small, agriculturally oriented areas, or the impact on water supply. These include impacts not immediately visible in the glossy 9" x 12" artist's conceptions of a plant; they involve new schools, more policemen, bigger hospitals.

The federal and state governments will continue to play a major role in industrial location, but I foresee a more creative approach with less emphasis on regulation. The laws and regulations already enacted are almost certainly firmly ensconced. Government, particularly the federal government, will be searching for ways to remove unnecessary roadblocks to development and to foster economic development, what many are calling the reindustrialization of America.

But the question is how can government be most effective? Some have suggested that this country emulate the Japanese approach where the government identifies likely growth industries and then tailors policies to promote them rather than sectors that appear to hold little growth potential. But making such predictions is very difficult. Most experts agree that we will not need many new oil refineries in the next decade, if any at all. Thus, the theory goes, the federal government would probably be wise not to push for such development in areas where there will be serious, adverse environmental impacts.

But the chemical industry demonstrates how dicey such predictions can be. Only a few years ago, experts predicted that the heady growth days for chemical firms in this country were over for reasons having little to do with environmental controls. Europe had a serious overcapacity and rapidly industrializing countries such as Brazil and Korea stood to capture a larger share of the international market for reasons unrelated to environmental regulation. Decontrol of oil prices in the United States was also seen as eroding the competitive advantage of U.S. firms. Before the recession hit the picture was mixed, but not dismal. Fertilizer demand was booming while the picture for polyester fibers was off. Should the government have then put proposals for new fertilizer plants on a fast track? Now, fertilizer demand is down along with farm prices.

The overall growth outlook for the five biggest pollution-intensive industries—rubber, primary metals, chemicals, pulp and paper, and oil refining—is rather poor. Thus, we are likely to see fewer battles over major industrial facilities such as Dow simply because fewer new ones will be built. Expansion rather than new construction is likely to be the norm. This fact, coupled with the inherent difficulty in choosing winners and losers among industries, indicates that the federal government will probably do better taking a less direct role. This does not mean sitting back and doing nothing. When a big plant is proposed, particularly an energy facility, the federal and state governments can help industry identify which sites are off-limits from an environmental or land-use point of view, those without a fighting chance for approval, and help local governments plan for and accommodate the growth that will come with these projects.

Governments can also play an important role in fostering the major growth we are likely to see in high technology sectors, such as computers and electronics, that are relatively pollution free. Instead of blunderbuss tax breaks for business such as accelerated depreciation allowances, which are of greatest benefit to large, capital-intensive, mature companies of the Fortune 500 variety, government may be wiser to focus incentives to spur growth of expanding smaller businesses that account for most new jobs in this country. Simply transferring cash to large, established companies won't guarantee that they will grow quickly. As one economist has noted, it's like trying to make gazelles out of dinosaurs by feeding them more. Reduction in capital gains taxes and other steps to encourage entrepreneurship may make more sense than tinkering with depreciation allowances.

But even these small businesses are not without environmental problems. There are serious indications that the early lead this country has taken in the computer field may be lost because, among several factors, localities cannot handle the growth problems that the exploding industry has brought with it. Santa Clara County in California, better known as "Silicon Valley," may be setting an example for other fast growing areas, particularly in the Sunbelt, that were until recently struggling with the problem of too many jobs.

There, business and government leaders are attempting to work out a plan to slow industrial growth so that the county can get a handle on its infrastructure and housing problems created by an influx of people vying for the 45,000 new jobs created in 1980 alone. With a total of 681,000 jobs, Santa Clara County has a housing shortage of 31,000 units. As a result, the median price of a home skyrocketed, the housing vacancy rate is down to 1.7 percent, and the influx of commuters is jamming county roads with 44,000 vehicles a day in an area with already poor air quality. The county is toying with the idea of a moratorium on industrial growth if it cannot get a hold on these serious problems. Some firms are already moving out to environmentally attractive areas in Oregon and Arizona that have cheaper housing.

Firms in many growth sectors of the future will thrive, economists tell us, only if they can avail themselves of the advantages of agglomeration—being close to similar firms. Yet, this expansion may be stifled and this country's world leadership in these fields lost to the likes of Japan if we cannot respond to the growth problems these expanding "clean" industries bring with them. Similarly, many jurisdictions will fight needed energy developments if potential adverse impacts, particularly secondary growth, cannot be mitigated. Thus, environmental quality and land-use regulations may be, ironically, the very prescription for keeping the growth industries healthy and the search for energy on track.

The Dow case also hinted at the role environmentalists and conservationists will have to play in the future. In a post mortem on the Dow debacle, one environmentalist quoted a lady who had turned up at the Dow hearings to question whether there was any real need served by making more petrochemicals to manufacture more things made out of plastic. "I don't think we're going to solve the problems of this country," she said, "by making crummy things." Some involved in the Dow case cited this as a profound observation. In reality, it reveals a naivete that environmentalists must help to overcome.

Ray Brubaker told me a little story that, I think, reflects the growing maturity among conservationists:

> Bill Press and I had been talking after the project was killed. He said he had been thinking how the chemical industry affects people's lives. It really came home to him when he went to the beach and was playing with a frisbee. He turned it over and noticed from the label that it was made of petrochemicals.

Of course, the world would hardly end if all frisbees suddenly vanished, but there is no doubt that we all like to crow about how worthless and cheap things made of plastic are, and what a waste of energy all that plastic stuff is when we have natural materials such as wood available. But we often fail to consider that chemical exports are second only to agricultural products among U.S. exports, thus helping to pay for many of the products, including oil, that we import. Should I give up my new plastic canoe for an aluminum or wood one even though the former is far superior in navigating the rapids I run on the Potomac River? Perhaps I must give up— my wife says God forbid—my beloved polyester/cotton no-iron shirts for 100 percent cotton ones. And maybe we should be using more wood and metal in cars instead of those plastic knobs, gadgets, and dials.

Not so, according to Christopher Flavin of an environmental think tank, the Worldwatch Institute. Flavin observes in a recent paper that "natural fibers, wood products, and metals as currently produced and processed often require large energy inputs, much of it derived from the same fossil fuels needed to provide feedstocks for the synthetics."[35] An aluminum canoe involves the processing of bauxite ore that requires huge amounts of electricity. That electricity is often generated by dams that have destroyed the rivers canoeists and conservationists fought to save. A study financed by the National Science Foundation says that while a polyester/cotton blend shirt takes only 25 percent more energy to produce than a cotton one, the polyester/cotton fabrics last longer and require less energy to maintain, thus actually saving energy in the long run, at least in this country.[36] And use of plastics in cars will help to reduce their overall weight, which means better gas mileage and a saving of energy.

Thus, environmentalists need to carefully focus their efforts on the profligate use of synthetics, like the plastic Christmas tree I saw standing in the reception room at the President's Council on Environmental Quality in December of 1980, or the wasteful over-packaging of products with plastics, or the outrageous driving habits of many Americans. Of course, they have done this already to a certain extent, leading the fight for the decontrol of oil prices so that gasoline consumption would not be subsidized through artificially low costs.

In many ways, the challenge for environmentalists is one of public and political education; to make people realize, for example, that it is the automobile that is responsible for air pollution problems in many cities, problems that if not remedied will mean no industrial growth. California and the San Francisco area are good cases in point. Dow Chemical faced a serious problem in building its new plant because the Bay Area does not meet federal ambient air standards for hydrocarbons. Cars are the major source of that hydrocarbon pollution; yet the California legislature, which has enacted a series of strong laws to make it tough on industrial polluters, has not imposed annual inspections of smog controls on automobiles. And we all continue to drive. As Jack Jones said, "I didn't see many environmentalists bicycling to the Dow hearings."

Again, environmentalists have taken the lead in pushing for fuel-efficient, less-polluting cars. But this push has taken place in an adversarial climate, albeit one created as much by industry as by environmentalists. What is needed now, more than ever, is for the debate on such issues to be a thoughtful one, not polarized, not characterized by diatribe nor marred by the sanctimonious attitude that some environmentalists often bring with them. Some far-seeing environmental leaders know that change is coming. The environmental laws enacted in the 1970s are not perfect and changes need to be made. With some justification, others fight any discussion of how things might be "reformed," especially when it comes to substantive standards, fearing that "reform" is a smokescreen for "gutting" by industry. The Reagan Administration has given them little reason for comfort.

Many conservationists recognize there are problems with laws like the Clean Air Act. Douglas Costle, head of EPA under the Carter Administration, had this to say in a speech entitled "The Clean Air Act—A Law In Trouble": "Despite the accomplishments of the Clean Air Act, it is a troublesome and complex statute . . . . The air quality management processs is difficult."[37] Costle recognized that some of the key standards upon which our regulatory systems for air pollution are based are flimsy simply because we lack sufficient scientific information, thus forcing regulators to rely on instinct, values, and personal judgment. He also explained that, in the context of ambient air standards, "the process of determining the right emission limits is amazingly difficult." That process involves, in Costle's words, "a huge number of highly uncertain explorations into modeling, monitoring and meteorological impacts, emissions inventories, and so on." Ironically, the Reagan Administration, which has waged a jihad against environmental controls, has also attempted to cut EPA's research capabilities that could help put many regulations on a firmer footing.

The changes this country must make in its environmental quality regulations will be difficult, which leads me to conclude that we all must face the fact that, as the *Washington Post* editorialized recently: "A great deal can be done to make government regulations more sensible, less expensive and more effective. But the sad truth is that, for many years to come, uncertainty and confusion will necessarily remain a large part of the process. There is just no way around it." A sobering message, but one that rings true.

Footnotes

1. Joan Didion, "Notes from a Native Daughter," *Slouching Towards Bethlehem* (New York: Farrar, Straus & Giroux), p. 171.

2. "Why Dow Continues to Make Napalm," *Business Week*, February 10, 1968, p. 124.3. *Los Angeles Times*, November 25, 1980.

3. *Los Angeles Times*, November 25, 1980.

4. The environmental impact analysis filed on the Dow project listed the following formal site selection criteria:

> a. The end-use market. The products are ultimately purchased and consumed by the population and hence proximity provides an efficient distribution of goods manufactured.
> b. Environmental impact. Ability to control air, water, and visual impacts consistent with appropriate zoning and safety requirements.
> c. Transportation means. Existing transportation systems and the economic and environmental impacts of competing methods of transportation.
> d. Land uses. The desirability of specific land uses for alternate purposes, i.e., agriculture, recreation, open space, etc.
> e. People resources. Ability to construct facilities, operate them, and continually improve them depends on competent, well-trained personnel.
> g. Population. The ability of the local communities to support the project personnel.

5. A.J. Piombino, "Dow: Profile of a Global Enterprise," *Chemical Week*, August 27, 1975, p. 23.

6. For an exposition of Storper's views regarding the Dow case, see Michael Storper, Robert Walker, and Ellen Widess, "Performance Regulation and Industrial Location: A Case Study," *Environment and Planning*, vol. 13 (1981), pp. 321-338.

7. According to Beckee Beemer, she was not actually in charge of all environmental permits. That job was the responsibility of David Bower. Ms. Beemer, who worked under Bower, did work on various aspects of environmental permits and coordinated land-use studies.

8. Jack London, *Tales of the Fish Patrol* (1905; reprinted. Plainview, N.Y.: Books for Libraries Press, 1976), p. 11.

9. See Bernard Frieden, *The Environmental Protection Hustle* (Cambridge, Mass.: MIT Press, 1979). Frieden's book has come under fire from environmentalists for being biased and unsupported by any hard economic data. Frieden himself admits that many other factors, such as high interest rates

and land speculation, contributed to rising housing costs.

10. Robert G. Healy and James L. Short, *The Market for Rural Land: Trends, Issues, Policies* (Washington, D.C.: The Conservation Foundation, 1981).

11. The California Land Conservation Act of 1965, *Cal. Govt. Code* Sec. 51200-295. For a good analysis of the act, see *The Property Tax and Open Space Preservation in California, A Study of the Williamson Act*, Stanford Environmental Law Society, 1974.

12. Seymour I. Schwartz, *et al.*, "Measures for Strengthening the California Land Conservation Act," a report to the California Legislature, Assembly, Select Committee on Open Space Land, December 1974.

13. Michael Storper and Barbara Des Rochers, "Can a Quiet Agricultural County on the Sacramento River Find True Happiness with a Huge, Messy Chemical Plant?" *Not Man Apart*, March 1976, p. 1.

14. Quoted in Anne Jackson, "Industry vs. Ecology Showdown: the $500 Million Dow Plant," *California Journal*, February 1977, p. 43.

15. Storper and Des Rochers, *op. cit.*

16. Storper and Des Rochers, *op. cit.*

17. Jackson, *op. cit.*, p. 46.

18. Jackson, *op. cit.*, p. 46.

19. These and some of the following comments by Mr. Press are from an interview appearing in the *Pacific Sun*, July 13-19, 1979, pp. 3-7.

20. "Clean Air Versus Jobs—A Case History," *Chemical Week*, October 27, 1976, p. 50.

21. Little was made of the fact that this modeling was one by the same consultant firm that employed Stephen Moore, who had testified for the Sierra Club.

22. C.A. Gerstacker, "Profits and Pollution," *Vital Speeches*, April 1, 1972, p. 368.

23. John Zierold, "The View From Sacramento" *Sierra*, June 1978, p. 16.

24. Orville Schell, *Brown* (New York: Random House, 1978), p. 229.

25. *Wall Street Journal*, July 12, 1977, p.1.

26. *Chemical and Engineering News*, September 11, 1978, p. 13.

27. Barry I. Castleman, *The Export of Hazardous Factories in Developing Nations* (Independent Report, March 7, 1978), p. 3. (Available from The Conservation Foundation.)

28. Quoted in *Environmental Reporter*, Volume 9, Number 10, July 7, 1979, p. 451.

29. An article by Eugene Leong, Charles Lewis IV, and Ronald Wada, entitled "The Role of New Source Review Policy: The San Francisco Air Quality Maintenance Plan," *Journal of the Air Pollution Control Association*, Volume 20, Number 4, April 1979, p. 340, provides a more detailed discussion of these changes.

30. The following quotes are from "Cancer Rate Spurs Anxiety in Industrial

Area Near San Francisco," *New York Times*, March 28, 1982, col. 1, p. 26.

31. A more comprehensive discussion of the lessons of Dow and other industrial siting disputes will appear in forthcoming publications from The Conservation Foundation's Industrial Siting Project.

32. The AMAX project, which was well on its way to securing approval, was temporarily postponed in early 1982 due to economic conditions.

33. *County of Suffolk v. Secretary of Interior*, 562 F.2d 1368 (2d Cir. 1977) (action may proceed on best available information); *Alaska v. Andrus*, 580 F.2d 465 (D.C. Cir. 1978) (no need to initiate special studies); *Hoe v. Alexander*, 483 F.Supp. 746 (D. Hawaii 1980) (remote and speculative consequences need not be discussed).

34. Quoted in Robert Mitchell, *Public Opinion on Environmental Issues* (Washington, D.C.: Council on Environmental Quality, 1980).

35. Christopher Flavin, "The Future of Synthetic Materials: The Petroleum Connection," Worldwatch Paper 36, April 1980.

36. T. Leo Van Winkle, *et al.*, "Cotton versus Polyester," *American Scientist*, May-June 1978.

37. Douglas Costle, "The Clean Air Act: A Law in Trouble?" *Journal of the Air Pollution Control Association*, August 1980, p. 844.

A Chronology

Fall, 1974	Dow conducts preliminary project studies and holds behind-the-scenes discussions with government officials about the proposal.
February, 1975	Dow announces it will build a 13-unit, $500-million petrochemical complex 35 miles northeast of San Francisco in Solano County.
August, 1975	Dow circulates a draft environmental impact report (EIR) on the project as required by state and federal laws. State and local agencies, given 30 days to review, sign off on EIR.
December, 1975	Solano County Board of Supervisors certifies that the EIR contains an adequate assessment of all environmental impacts and that the project will have no significant adverse environmental effects. Dow exercises option to buy land for the project. Solano County Board of Supervisors then cancels a Williamson Act contract on Dow's property and rezones a portion of the site from agricultural to industrial.
December 19, 1975	Environmental organizations sue Solano County and Dow, challenging various aspects of the project and local government actions approving it.
March, 1976	State agencies begin voicing concerns about the Dow project. The California Office of Planning and Research (OPR) holds a public technical briefing on the project.

145

April, 1976

The U.S. Army Corps of Engineers issues a draft environmental impact statement (EIS) for the project as required by federal law.

May 4, 1976

Dow submits applications for air pollution permits with the regional Bay Area Air Pollution Control District (BAAPCD).

June, 1976

The California Resources Agency sends a formal 14-page letter to the U.S. Army Corps of Engineers objecting to the project.

July 8, 1976

BAAPCD issues a preliminary denial of Dow's application for air pollution permits.

August 12, 1976

BAAPCD reaffirms its earlier denial of air pollution permits.

August, 1976

Ray Brubaker replaces Al Look as head of Dow's Western Division with a mandate to get the project moving. Brubaker immediately files an appeal of BAAPCD's denial of air pollution permits.

September, 1976

Brubaker and other Dow officials meet with Governor Jerry Brown and several cabinet members in an attempt to get a speedy "yes" or "no" decision on the project. Brown agrees to hold consolidated state hearings.

Fall, 1976

In a series of public hearings, Dow presents its case on appeal of BAAPCD's denial of air pollution permits.

December, 1976

Bill Press oversees several days of hearings by state agencies that have permit authority over the Dow project.

January 18, 1977

Dow cancels its proposed petrochemical project.

The Players

Stan and Louise Anderson. A Solano County farm family that opposed Dow.

Nick Arguimbau. A young Environmental Defense Fund lawyer who helped Larry Silver in the legal battle with Dow.

Beckee Beamer. Helped coordinate environmental reviews and studies for Dow's project.

Richard Brann. Chairman of the Solano County Board of Supervisors in 1975-1976 and a strong proponent of the proposed chemical facility.

Ray Brubaker. A Dow official who replaced Al Look as head of the Western Division in 1976 when the project faltered.

D. J. (Jud) Callaghan. Executive head of the Bay Area Air Pollution Control District (BAAPCD) in 1974-1976.

Claire Dedrick. Top official at the California Resources Agency during the Dow dispute.

Paul DeFalco. Ran the U.S. EPA's regional office in San Francisco during the Dow dispute.

Bill and Leslie Emmington. Collinsville property owners who spearheaded local opposition to Dow.

Milton Feldstein. Second in command in 1974-1976 at the Bay Area Air Pollution Control District.

Jerry Gilbert. A former state official who was hired as a consultant by Dow to prepare the environmental impact statement for the project.

Al Gunkler. The chief engineer on Dow's proposed project.

Jack Jones. A Dow official who helped coordinate government relations and obtain environmental permits for Dow's proposed chemical facility.

Cynthia Kay. A Vallejo environmentalist who was one of Dow's staunchest opponents.

Larry King. An attorney in the California Attorney General's environmental unit assigned to the Dow project.

Al Look. Head of the Western Division when the project was conceived. Later bumped aside when the project bogged down in 1976.

Neil Moyer. An official at the state Air Resources Board who raised questions about air pollution from the proposed Dow facility.

McOmie. The Solano County farmer from whom Dow bought land for its chemical refinery.

Clayne Munk. Head of the Solano County Planning Department.

Paul Oreffice. President of Dow U.S.A. in 1976; later elevated to head the entire company.

Bob Perry. An engineer at Dow who coordinated various aspects of the proposal.

Bill Press. Head of the California Governor's Office of Planning and Research during the Dow dispute.

Art Shelton. Dow's local lawyer.

Clem Shute. High-ranking lawyer in the California Attorney General's environmental unit.

Larry Silver. A Sierra Club attorney who filed suit to stop the Dow project.

Michael Storper. A University of California geographer who joined with Arguimbau and Kay to oppose Dow.

Joe Vitale. A retired Collinsville fisherman.

Ellen Widess. A member of Friends of the Earth who lived in Contra Costa County and worked against Dow's proposed facility.

Tom Willoughby. Top staffer on the California Assembly Committee on Resources, Land & Energy who authored many provisions of AB 884, which was enacted to remedy problems that arose in the Dow controversy.

Evelle Younger. California Attorney General during the Dow controversy.

Names of Organizations and Agencies

U.S. GOVERNMENT AGENCIES

Environmental Protection Agency. Created in 1970 as an independent federal agency to oversee administration of national air and water pollution laws and regulations.

U.S. Army Corps of Engineers. Given authority under several federal laws to regulate dredging and filling of navigable waters and wetlands.

Council on Environmental Quality. A small executive agency created in the early 1970s to advise the President on environmental issues.

CALIFORNIA STATE AGENCIES AND LOCAL GOVERNMENTS

Air Resources Board. An independent state agency charged with coordinating efforts to attain air quality standards in California. Directly responsible for controlling vehicle emissions, but only indirect authority over industry facilities.

Office of Planning and Research. California's statewide planning agency that reports directly to the Governor. It focuses on land-use, housing, and natural resource policy and coordinates objectives and procedures for environmental impact reports.

Resources Agency. A state superagency that supervises and coordinates other state environmental agencies such as the Air Resources Board, the Coastal Commission, and others.

Solano County Planning Department. County land-use agency responsible for reviewing zoning and development proposals. Lead agency in preparing Dow environmental impact report required by state law.

Bay Area Air Pollution Control District (BAAPCD). Independent

149

regional agency with regulatory authority over industrial pollution sources in the San Francisco region, including Solano County. Name later changed to Bay Area Air Quality Management District (BAAQMD).

Office of Business and Economic Development. Part of the larger Business and Transportation agency with responsibility to promote economic growth in the state.

Department of Food and Agriculture. In the field of environmental protection, the department oversees administration of the agricultural lands protection (Williamson) act and conducts surveys regarding plant damage caused by air pollution.

San Francisco Bay Conservation and Development Commission (BCDC). Created in 1965, BCDC has regulatory authority over all dredging and filling in San Francisco Bay (including San Pablo and Suisun Bays) and controls development within 100 feet of the Bay.

Water Resources Control Board. Allocates water rights, administers water appropriation laws, and coordinates regional water quality control boards which have regulatory authority over water effluent discharges.

A List of Acronyms

AB	Assembly Bill
ABAG	Association of Bay Area Governments
ARB	California Air Resource Board
ARCO	Atlantic Richfield Company
BAAPCD	Bay Area Air Pollution Control District
BCDC	Bay Area Conservation and Development Commission
CEQA	California Environmental Quality Act
CJRP	Colorado joint review process
COLAB	Coalition of Labor and Business
EIR	environmental impact review
EIS	environmental impact statement
EPA	U.S. Environmental Protection Agency
LNG	liquified natural gas
NEPA	National Environmental Policy Act
OPR	Office of Planning and Research
OSHA	Occupational Safety and Health Administration
PCL	Planning and Conservation League
PG&E	Pacific Gas & Electric Company
SRI	SRI International, formerly the Stanford Research Institute
UAW	United Auto Workers Union